Edexcel GCSE (9-1)

# History

Russia and the Soviet Union, 1917–1941

Series Editor: Angela Leonard   Author: Martyn Whittock

ALWAYS LEARNING

**PEARSON**

Published by Pearson Education Limited, 80 Strand, London, WC2R 0RL.

www.pearsonschoolsandfecolleges.co.uk

Copies of official specifications for all Edexcel qualifications may be found on the website: www.edexcel.com

Text © Pearson Education Limited 2016

Series editor: Angela Leonard
Designed by Colin Tilley Loughrey, Pearson Education Limited
Typeset by Phoenix Photosetting, Chatham, Kent
Original illustrations © Pearson Education Limited
Illustrated by KJA Artists Illustration Agency and Phoenix Photosetting, Chatham, Kent.

Cover design by Colin Tilley Loughrey
Picture research by Ewout Buckens
Cover photo © Bridgeman Art Library Ltd: National Portrait Gallery, London, UK

The right of Martyn Whittock to be identified as author of this work has been asserted by her in accordance with the Copyright, Designs and Patents Act 1988.

First published 2016

19 18 17 16
10 9 8 7 6 5 4 3 2 1

British Library Cataloguing in Publication Data
A catalogue record for this book is available from the British Library.
ISBN 978 1 292 12729 3

Printed in the UK by CPI, UK

**A note from the publisher**
In order to ensure that this resource offers high-quality support for the associated Pearson qualification, it has been through a review process by the awarding body. This process confirms that this resource fully covers the teaching and learning content of the specification or part of a specification at which it is aimed. It also confirms that it demonstrates an appropriate balance between the development of subject skills, knowledge and understanding, in addition to preparation for assessment.

Endorsement does not cover any guidance on assessment activities or processes (e.g. practice questions or advice on how to answer assessment questions), included in the resource nor does it prescribe any particular approach to the teaching or delivery of a related course.

While the publishers have made every attempt to ensure that advice on the qualification and its assessment is accurate, the official specification and associated assessment guidance materials are the only authoritative source of information and should always be referred to for definitive guidance.

Pearson examiners have not contributed to any sections in this resource relevant to examination papers for which they have responsibility.

Examiners will not use endorsed resources as a source of material for any assessment set by Pearson.

Endorsement of a resource does not mean that the resource is required to achieve this Pearson qualification, nor does it mean that it is the only suitable material available to support the qualification, and any resource lists produced by the awarding body shall include this and other appropriate resources.

**Websites**
Pearson Education Limited is not responsible for the content of any external internet sites. It is essential for tutors to preview each website before using it in class so as to ensure that the URL is still accurate, relevant and appropriate. We suggest that tutors bookmark useful websites and consider enabling students to access them through the school/college intranet.

# Contents

# How to use this book

## What's covered?

This book covers the Modern Depth study on Russia and the Soviet Union, 1917–41. This unit makes up 30% of your GCSE course, and will be examined in Paper 3.

Modern depth studies cover a short period of time, and require you to know about a society or historical situation in detail. You need to understand different aspects within this period, such as social, economic, political, cultural and military aspects, and how they interact with each other. This book also explains the different types of exam questions you will need to answer, and includes advice and example answers to help you improve.

## Features

As well as a clear, detailed explanation of the key knowledge you will need, you will also find a number of features in the book:

### Key terms

Where you see a word followed by an asterisk, like this: Militia*, you will be able to find a Key Terms box on that page that explains what the word means.

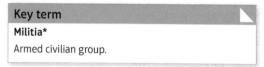

**Key term**

**Militia***
Armed civilian group.

### Activities

Every few pages, you'll find a box containing some activities designed to help check and embed knowledge and get you to really think about what you've studied. The activities start simple, but might get more challenging as you work through them.

### Summaries and Checkpoints

At the end of each chunk of learning, the main points are summarised in a series of bullet points – great for embedding the core knowledge, and handy for revision.

Checkpoints help you to check and reflect on your learning. The Strengthen section helps you to consolidate knowledge and understanding, and check that you've grasped the basic ideas and skills. The Challenge questions push you to go beyond just understanding the information, and into evaluation and analysis of what you've studied.

## Sources and Interpretations

This book contains numerous contemporary pictorial and text sources that show what people from the period, said, thought or created.

The book also includes extracts from the work of historians, showing how experts have interpreted the events you've been studying.

You will need to be comfortable examining both sources and interpretations to answer questions in your Paper 3 exam.

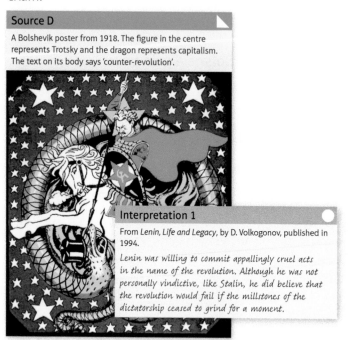

**Source D**

A Bolshevik poster from 1918. The figure in the centre represents Trotsky and the dragon represents capitalism. The text on its body says 'counter-revolution'.

**Interpretation 1**

From *Lenin, Life and Legacy*, by D. Volkogonov, published in 1994.

*Lenin was willing to commit appallingly cruel acts in the name of the revolution. Although he was not personally vindictive, like Stalin, he did believe that the revolution would fail if the millstones of the dictatorship ceased to grind for a moment.*

## Extend your knowledge

These features contain useful additional information that adds depth to your knowledge, and to your answers. The information is closely related to the key issues in the unit, and questions are sometimes included, helping you to link the new details to the main content.

**Extend your knowledge**

**Stalin's nickname**

Stalin's real name was Joseph Vissarionovich Dzhugashvili. 'Stalin' was his nickname: which means 'man of steel'. He started using this alternative name before 1914. It later turned out to be doubly appropriate: he was a hard man and, also, under him the iron and steel production in the Soviet Union increased enormously.

## Exam-style questions and tips

The book also includes extra exam-style questions you can use to practise. These appear in the chapters and are accompanied by a tip to help you get started on an answer.

> **Exam-style question, Section B** ⚪
>
> How useful are Sources B and C for an enquiry into the living standards of citizens of the Soviet Union in the 1930s?
>
> Explain your answer, using Sources B and C and your knowledge of the historical context.  **8 marks**

> **Exam tip** ⚪
>
> First identify the impression you get from each source, then explain what they are useful for, and any limits to their use. Finally, compare the information in them to what else you know about the situation in the 1930s, to assess their accuracy or completeness.

## Recap pages

At the end of each chapter, you'll find a page designed to help you to consolidate and reflect on the chapter as a whole. Each recap page includes a recall quiz, ideal for quickly checking your knowledge or for revision. Recap pages also include activities designed to help you summarise and analyse what you've learned, and also reflect on how each chapter links to other parts of the unit.

## THINKING HISTORICALLY

These activities are designed to help you develop a better understanding of how history is constructed, and are focused on the key areas of Evidence, Interpretations, Cause & Consequence and Change & Continuity. In the Modern Depth Study, you will come across activities on Cause & Consequence, Evidence and Interpretations as these are key areas of focus for this unit.

The Thinking Historically approach has been developed in conjunction with Dr Arthur Chapman and the Institute of Education, UCL. It is based on research into the misconceptions that can hold students back in history.

THINKING HISTORICALLY ▷ Cause and Consequence (3c&d) ⟶ conceptual map reference

The Thinking Historically conceptual map can be found at: www.pearsonschools.co.uk/thinkinghistoricallygcse

## WRITING HISTORICALLY

At the end of most chapters is a spread dedicated to helping you improve your writing skills. These include simple techniques you can use in your writing to make your answers clearer, more precise and better focused on the question you're answering.

The Writing Historically approach is based on the *Grammar for Writing* pedagogy developed by a team at the University of Exeter and popular in many English departments. Each spread uses examples from the preceding chapter, so it's relevant to what you've just been studying.

## Preparing for your exams

At the back of the book, you'll find a special section dedicated to explaining and exemplifying the new Edexcel GCSE History exams. Advice on the demands of this paper, written by Angela Leonard, helps you prepare for and approach the exam with confidence. Each question type is explained through annotated sample answers at two levels, showing clearly how answers can be improved.

**Pearson Progression Scale:** This icon indicates the Step that a sample answer has been graded at on the Pearson Progression Scale.

*This book is also available as an online ActiveBook, which can be licensed for your whole institution.*

*There is also an ActiveLearn Digital Service available to support delivery of this book, featuring a front-of-class version of the book, lesson plans, worksheets, exam practice PowerPoints, assessments, notes on Thinking Historically and Writing Historically, and more.*

## ActiveLearn
Digital Service

# Timeline: Russia and the Soviet Union, 1917–41

**1914–18**
First World War

**1917**
Jan–Feb: Mass protests in Petrograd against rule of Tsar Nicholas II and the problems caused by First World War

**1917**
March: Duma Committee establishes Provisional Government; Nicholas II abdicates

**1917**
April: Lenin returns from exile

**1917**
July: Kerensky takes control of Provisional Government

**1917**
August: Kornilov Revolt

**1921**
March: Kronstadt Mutiny; 10th Party Congress – Workers' Opposition and 'factionalism' banned

**1923**
Scissors Crisis

**1927**
Stalin defeats United Opposition in power struggle; war scare; start of grain shortages

**1928**
Start of First Five-Year Plan; start of collectivisation

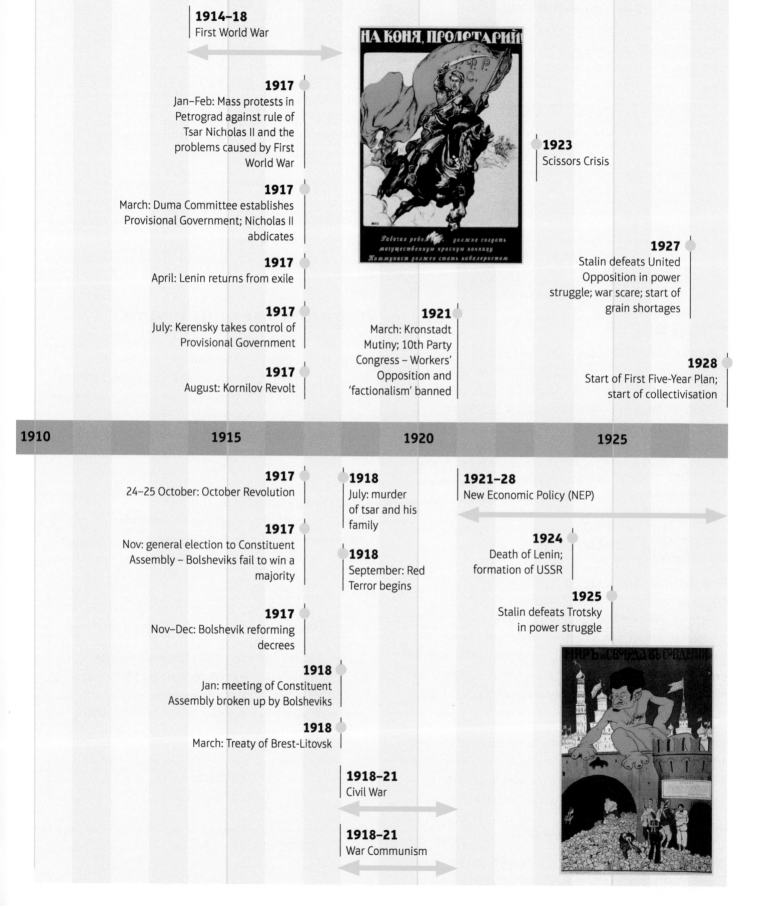

| 1910 | 1915 | 1920 | 1925 |
|------|------|------|------|

**1917**
24–25 October: October Revolution

**1917**
Nov: general election to Constituent Assembly – Bolsheviks fail to win a majority

**1917**
Nov–Dec: Bolshevik reforming decrees

**1918**
Jan: meeting of Constituent Assembly broken up by Bolsheviks

**1918**
March: Treaty of Brest-Litovsk

**1918–21**
Civil War

**1918–21**
War Communism

**1918**
July: murder of tsar and his family

**1918**
September: Red Terror begins

**1921–28**
New Economic Policy (NEP)

**1924**
Death of Lenin; formation of USSR

**1925**
Stalin defeats Trotsky in power struggle

**1932**
Stalin cannot persuade Politburo to
have Ryutin shot; internal passports
introduced

**1939**
Labour camp population
reaches around seven
million

**1933**
Start of Second Five-Year Plan;
collectivisation famine

**1934**
Murder of Kirov

**1941**
German invasion of USSR

**1935**
Start of Stakhanovite Movement

| 1930 | 1935 | 1940 | 1945 |
|------|------|------|------|

**1929**
Stalin defeats Bukharin to win power
struggle; start of liquidation of kulaks

**1936**
Stalin tells NKVD they are four years
behind in search for 'enemies'; first
show trials – Zinoviev and Kamenev
shot; new Soviet Constitution

**1930**
Zhenotdel (women's section of
Communist Party) closed down

**1937**
Start of 'Yezhovschina';
purge of the military

**1938**
Last show trial – Bukharin is
shot; Yezhov arrested; start
of Third Five-Year Plan

**1939–45**
Second World War

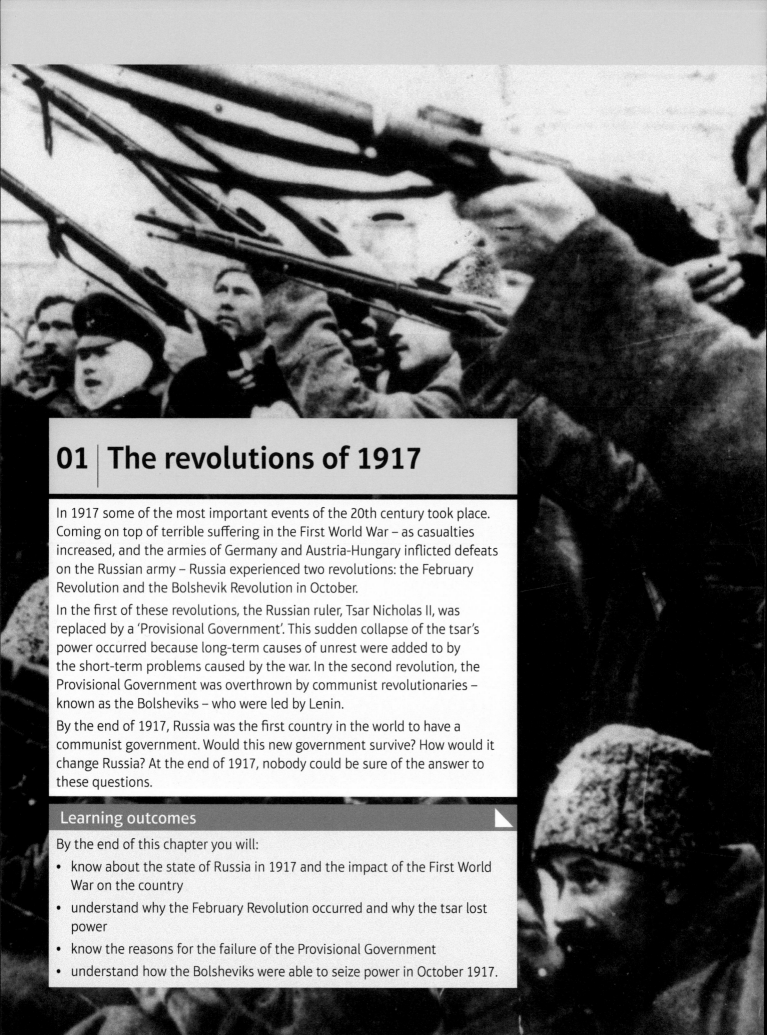

# 01 | The revolutions of 1917

In 1917 some of the most important events of the 20th century took place. Coming on top of terrible suffering in the First World War – as casualties increased, and the armies of Germany and Austria-Hungary inflicted defeats on the Russian army – Russia experienced two revolutions: the February Revolution and the Bolshevik Revolution in October.

In the first of these revolutions, the Russian ruler, Tsar Nicholas II, was replaced by a 'Provisional Government'. This sudden collapse of the tsar's power occurred because long-term causes of unrest were added to by the short-term problems caused by the war. In the second revolution, the Provisional Government was overthrown by communist revolutionaries – known as the Bolsheviks – who were led by Lenin.

By the end of 1917, Russia was the first country in the world to have a communist government. Would this new government survive? How would it change Russia? At the end of 1917, nobody could be sure of the answer to these questions.

## Learning outcomes

By the end of this chapter you will:

- know about the state of Russia in 1917 and the impact of the First World War on the country
- understand why the February Revolution occurred and why the tsar lost power
- know the reasons for the failure of the Provisional Government
- understand how the Bolsheviks were able to seize power in October 1917.

# 1.1  Russia in early 1917

**Learning outcomes**

- Understand the political situation in Russia in early 1917, and why many sectors of society were unhappy with the government.
- Know what the main opposition groups were, and what changes they wanted to see in Russia.
- Understand the impact the First World War had on the political situation in Russia.

In February 1917, a revolution overthrew Tsar Nicholas II, ending 400 years of rule over Russia by the Romanov dynasty. This started a chain reaction of changes which eventually led to the Bolsheviks* seizing power in October 1917. Before looking at the revolutions of 1917 (in Sections 1.2–1.4), this section explores the background to these events.

## Threats to the tsarist government

Tsar Nicholas had a large army, and also used his secret police force, the Okhrana, to maintain power. The Russian parliament (called the duma) found it difficult to challenge the tsar, and workers found it difficult to organise trade unions. Richer peasants*, in the countryside, generally supported their 'Little Father' – as the tsar was often called. The tsar's position looked reasonably strong.

Yet, by the winter of 1916–17, his rule was increasingly under threat – and in February 1917 he was overthrown. A royal family that had ruled Russia since the 17th century lost power – and Russia became a republic*. What were the events that led to the overthrow of the tsarist regime*?

### Reasons for discontent in 1917

Although, in early 1917, the tsar seemed in a powerful position, there were many reasons why both peasants and town workers were discontented with the way that Russia was run. These reasons had been building up for some time, and were long-term causes of the anger that brought down the tsar in 1917.

#### The peasants

In 1917, about 80% of the Russian population were peasants.

**Key terms**

**Bolsheviks***

A dedicated group of communist revolutionaries led by Lenin.

**Peasants***

Farmers who work a small area of land. Most of the Russian population, at this time, were peasants.

**Republic***

A country without a king or a queen ruling over it.

**Regime***

A government – the way a country is ruled.

Most peasant communities were very backward, and the farming methods available to them were inefficient. Modern farming equipment was unknown, and wooden horse-drawn ploughs were still in use. Houses lacked running water and flushing toilets. In many homes, animals were kept at one end of the building, while the humans lived at the other. Most peasants, especially women and older people, were illiterate.

Almost all peasants wished to see wealthy landowners lose their land and have it redistributed among the ordinary peasants. Most also resented the interference of government and wanted it to leave them alone to get on with their lives. There was a tradition of peasant uprisings against landlords and government officials. This made the peasants a dangerously violent group in society who might, at times of difficulty or unhappiness, turn to violence.

When the First World War broke out in 1918 the situation for Russian peasants became even more difficult (see page 14).

9

**Kulaks**
Better-off peasants who owned enough land to make a reasonable living and live in a more comfortable house. In Russian, 'kulak' means 'fist' or 'grasping' and reveals how less well-off peasants in the villages resented the richer peasants.

**Middle peasants**
Owned a small amount of land and lived in the villages.

**Poor peasants**
Did not own any land. Hired themselves out as labourers on the farms of their wealthier neighbours.

**Figure 1.1** The different classes of Russian peasant.

## Source A

A peasant family outside their one-room log hut in the Gorno-altai region, Siberia. This photograph was taken in 1912.

In shops and markets there were food shortages – not so much because less food was being grown, but because peasants were tending to hoard it. As prices went up for manufactured goods, peasants hung onto their grain, partly to try and force up the price, and partly to make sure they had enough food for themselves.

### Town workers

Life for workers* in the cities was also very difficult. Living conditions were often poor, with workers living in overcrowded barracks and slums*. Many Russian cities had grown so quickly in the years before the First World War that workers' houses were badly built and poorer areas were overcrowded. Petrograd (now St. Petersburg), which was the capital until 1918, almost tripled in size between 1881 and 1917. Moscow, which became the capital in 1918, more than doubled in size in the same time.

> ### Key terms
>
> **Worker***
>
> Man or woman employed in industries like steel works, textile mills, mines etc. They are also referred to as 'industrial workers'. Communist writers called workers the 'proletariat' and this word is often seen on communist posters.
>
> **Slum***
>
> Poor area of a city with low-quality overcrowded housing, lack of clean water and no waste disposal.

The tsar's police made it difficult for workers to form trade unions to campaign for better wages and conditions. Soldiers were often sent to end strikes or put down any unrest among the workers. This meant that even strikes about pay and conditions could easily turn into a confrontation between workers and the tsar's government.

Only a minority of people (less than 20% of the population) lived in towns away from the great cities of Petrograd, Moscow and eastern Ukraine – as most of the country had almost no industry. However, many Russian workers were employed in very large factories, such as the Putilov Steelworks in Petrograd. So, if the workers protested, it would have little effect on the country as a whole, but could cause massive disruption in the capital.

The war added to the workers' problems. Inflation* meant that prices went up faster than wages. Between 1914 and 1917, average wages went up by 200%, but the price of food and fuel went up by 400%. In other words, the living standard for workers in the town was cut by half. In addition, there was less food in the shops. So, at the start of 1917, workers were cold and hungry.

> ### Key term
>
> **Inflation***
>
> When prices rise and money buys less than it used to.

> ### Source B
>
> Women working in an industrial laundry, painted by the Russian artist Abram Efimovich Arkhipov in 1917.
>
>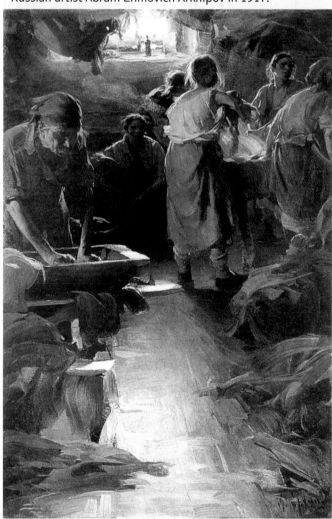

11

### Activities ?

1. In a small group, look carefully at Sources A and B. What do the images tell you about the quality of life of Russian peasants and workers? For each point you make, say what detail from the sources supports your point.
2. Using Sources A and B, and other information you have read so far, discuss why there was long-term discontent in Russia.
3. Discuss why the First World War caused workers and peasants to feel even more discontented with life in Russia by 1917.

## Organised opposition

There were a number of groups who were pressing for changes in Russia. Some of these were quite moderate and hoped that Russia might develop into a democracy – like France, the USA or Britain. These included liberal parties such as the Octobrists and the Kadets.

But, in contrast, there were also 'right wing' groups, such as the nationalists – who believed that Russians should be the leading group within a strong Russian empire – and the conservatives, who opposed social change.

On the 'left wing' were those who wanted to challenge the power of the rich. They included the Socialist Revolutionaries (SRs). Socialists believe in sharing out wealth to make a more equal society. Since the SRs promised to take land away from the great landowners and give it to the peasants, they had a lot of peasant support. By 1917, the SRs were really a collection of different left-wing groups rather than a united party. Their most revolutionary members were the 'Left SRs', who believed in revolutionary action and the assassination of 'political enemies' in the ruling class.

Also on the left were the Social Democrats. These were socialists (who also sometimes called themselves communists) who believed in the ideas of the German writer Karl Marx (died 1883). They thought that history was decided by struggle between different classes in society; and that, eventually, the workers (or proletariat) would rise up in revolution and overthrow the capitalist owners of industry. They believed this would lead to a fairer, communist society – with no more conflict between classes.

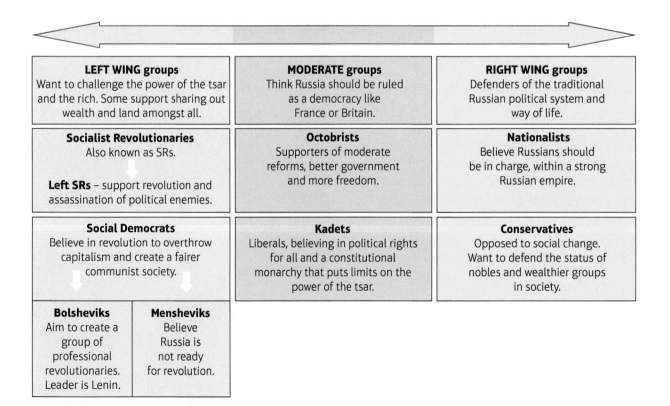

**Figure 1.2** The main political parties in Russia in 1917.

In 1903, the Social Democrats had split into two separate groups: the Mensheviks and the Bolsheviks. The Mensheviks thought Russia was not ready for revolution, and wanted to build a mass party involving many workers and revolutionaries. They were fairly democratic. In contrast, the Bolsheviks – led by Lenin – believed in forming a tight-knit group of professional revolutionaries who would not co-operate with other political parties. They were **not** democratic – and were tightly controlled by Lenin and their Central Committee.

In 1917, the Bolshevik leaders were in exile. Because they were against Russia's involvement in the First World War, they were accused of being traitors working for Germany. Lenin ended up in Switzerland. Some Mensheviks opposed the war too, while others thought it was right to defend Russia, as did many SRs.

## Extend your knowledge

### Revolutionaries in exile

Many of the leaders of the Russian revolutionary groups that opposed the tsar spent years in exile. Some were made to live in Siberia where the weather and living conditions were very harsh and challenging. Others were forced to leave Russia – by the tsarist police – and live abroad, or fled abroad to escape arrest. The Bolshevik leaders Lenin, Stalin and Trotsky all spent time in exile abroad.

# The impacts of the First World War on Russia

The First World War was one of the most terrible in history. By 1917, it had been dragging on for three bloody years, and had caused the deaths of millions of soldiers and civilians. Many of the countries fighting it were exhausted by its terrible effects. While Russia was the only country that faced revolution in that year, it was not the only country that was struggling to keep going in the face of enormous casualties and the demands of a war that affected all areas of society. The war impacted on Russia in a number of important ways.

## Military defeats

When the war started, in August 1914, the Russian government was confident that its enormous army would inflict defeats on its enemies – Germany and Austria-Hungary. They were to be disappointed. After early advances, Russian forces were defeated by the Germans.

By 1917, large areas of the Russian empire in the west were lost. The German army overran all of Russian Poland and Lithuania and most of Latvia.

**Figure 1.3** Impacts of the First World War on Russia.

**Key**
**Eastern front 1914–18**
– – – Farthest Russian advance 1914
••••• Front at time of Russian revolution 1917
– – – Farthest Austro-German advance 1918

**Figure 1.4** The Eastern Front, 1914–1918, where fighting took place between Russia and its enemies – Germany and Austria-Hungary.

## Economic effects of the war

The war was very expensive for Russia; and paying for it caused problems for ordinary Russians.

| Actions of the government | Economic problems this caused |
|---|---|
| Printed too much money (rouble notes). | Made paper money worth less – leading to inflation and increased cost of living. |
| Between 1914 and 1917, spent over 17,000 million roubles on the war. | Taxes went up to pay for government spending – which hit ordinary people hard. |
| Government's overall spending increased by eight times between 1913 and 1916. | Russia fell into debt as the government borrowed huge amounts of money from other countries. |

## Social effects of the war

The war led to an increase in social problems in towns and cities, which increased demands for a more equal society.

In 1916, food shortages grew worse when the army took control of railways and roads and took large amounts of food to feed the army. The Russian railway system virtually collapsed under the pressure of moving huge numbers of soldiers, and the food supply to towns and cities suffered.

The situation was particularly bad in Petrograd, which was far from food-producing areas. It was also struggling to cope with the many refugees who made their way there from other areas affected by the war. In January 1916, the daily bread ration was 1.2 kilograms; by early 1917 this had fallen to 0.8 kilograms – and poorer people in Petrograd were starving.

The same was true in other large cities. Before 1914, 2,200 waggons of grain a month had arrived in Moscow; by February 1917, this had fallen to fewer than 700.

The First World War brought unhappiness and suffering to the countryside too. Over 15 million peasant men fought in the Russian army leading to a massive loss of manpower. Many horses were seized by the military to haul guns and waggons. This had a huge impact on farms where horses were used for ploughing. It became harder to get hold of chemical fertilisers as industry was focused on making explosives and weapons. All this contributed further to the decline in food production in town and country alike.

## Political effects of the war

The duma (Russian parliament) did not support the tsar, after being side-lined in the running of the war. The tsar had dissolved the duma in 1914, in an attempt to get Russia behind his government and ensure there was no criticism of how the war was being run. In 1915, military defeats and criticism of the government forced the tsar to allow the duma to meet again. The duma asked the tsar to replace his advisers and ministers with new ones – supported by the duma – but the tsar refused. Had he agreed, he could have shared responsibility for the war and gained support within the duma – instead, by 1917, the duma became a centre of opposition to his government.

### *The tsar as commander-in-chief*

The tsar's position was dramatically weakened after he took personal command of the army in September

1915. The tsar's advisers reminded him that he had no practical experience of warfare, or of commanding armies in combat – but he ignored their advice and made himself commander-in-chief.

The tsar had little actual impact on the running of the war, since he usually did as his generals suggested; but, as commander-in-chief, he was personally blamed for the army's defeats. His new role also meant that he was usually at army headquarters and rarely in the capital; so when things started to go wrong in Petrograd, in February 1917, he was not there to take charge. If he had been in the capital, things may have gone the same way, but the situation was out of control before he could return to the city. He was isolated from the real centre of danger: his own disillusioned soldiers and the people of Petrograd.

Tsar Nicholas's decision to take charge of the army was one of his most serious mistakes – but it would not have mattered if the Russian army had been successful. So it's important to link this mistake with the fact that the army was poorly trained and poorly led by its generals.

The war severely weakened the tsar's rule, and lost him the respect and support of many who would otherwise have supported him. When the revolt of early 1917 came, there was virtually nobody ready to come to his assistance. The tsar had put himself into a dangerously isolated position.

## Interpretation 1

From *The Russian Revolution 1917-32*, by S. Fitzpatrick, published in 1982.

*The First World War both exposed and increased the vulnerability of Russia's old regime. The public applauded victories, but would not tolerate defeats. When defeats occurred, the society did not rally behind its government... but instead turned sharply against it, denouncing its incompetence and backwardness. This suggests that the regime's legitimacy [right to rule] had become extremely shaky, and that its survival was very closely related to visible achievements or, failing that, sheer luck... The war lasted too long, draining not only Russia but the whole of Europe. More than a year before the Armistice [end of fighting on 11 November 1918] in Europe, Russia's old regime was dead.*

## Activities ?

1 In pairs study Interpretation 1. 'Score' the First World War for how badly it affected Russia according to this source (1=little impact, 5=huge impact). Then write a sentence explaining your 'score'.

2 According to Sheila Fitzpatrick, in what ways did the First World War weaken the tsar's hold on power? Make a list of ways that it did so, using information from the interpretation.

3 From all the evidence that you have seen so far, does the evidence support Interpretation 1's view of the way the war impacted on Russia? Write a paragraph summing up your answer.

## Source C

Russian army conditions in the First World War.

## Exam-style question, Section A

Explain why the tsar's rule ended in early 1917. You may use the following in your answer:

- peasants and workers
- political parties

You **must** also use information of your own. **12 marks**

## Exam tip

This question is looking at causation. A good answer will go beyond describing the problems, to explaining why these brought an end to the rule of the tsar.

## Summary

- Russia faced problems in how it was run and organised in 1917.
- The rule of the tsar was already being challenged.
- These long-term problems were made worse by the effects of the war.
- Mistakes made by the tsar added to these problems; and by early 1917 his rule had been seriously weakened.

## Checkpoint

### Strengthen

**S1** Close the book and draw a spidergram showing the problems facing Russia in 1917. Colour code it to show political, economic, social and military problems. When you have finished, open these pages again and update your spidergram if you need to.

**S2** What do you think was the greatest threat facing the rule of the tsar by early 1917?

### Challenge

**C1** In your own words, summarise reasons for discontent amongst Russian workers in 1917.

**C2** In your own words, summarise reasons for discontent amongst Russian peasants in 1917.

**C3** Explain the political beliefs of the Bolsheviks.

How confident do you feel about your answers to these questions? If you're not sure you answered them well, share ideas with a neighbour and see what they think.

# 1.2 The February Revolution

## Learning outcomes

- Understand the short-term causes of the February Revolution.
- Know the role of important groups and individuals in the February Revolution.
- Know the main events of the February Revolution.

In February 1917, the tsarist government collapsed in a matter of days as the result of a sudden combination of events. Some of these were long-term causes: such as the long-standing discontent felt by peasants and workers that dated from before the First World War. Others were shorter-term causes that had been mounting since 1914: people were growing increasingly dissatisfied with the way the tsar's government was running the war, the high rate of casualties, and the impact of the war on the lives of civilians. Then there were what we might call 'trigger causes': these were the final combination of events which caused all these other 'causes' to explode into a challenge that was too great for the tsar's government to withstand.

## Triggers for revolt

Over the winter of 1916–17, food shortages and unrest among workers caused tensions to increase in the two great cities of Russia: the capital Petrograd and the second city, Moscow.

The final event, or 'trigger', for revolution was International Women's Day, on 23 February. Shortage of bread was causing hunger and desperation in many families. Bread shortages were made worse by strikes in some city bakeries, and also by peasants holding onto their grain in the hope of getting better prices for it. It was this shortage of food that brought thousands of women out onto the streets of Petrograd. The demonstration combined with short-term causes to spark revolution.

## Short-term causes of revolution in Petrograd in February 1917

The 'trigger event', of 23 February 1917, had such a dramatic effect because it accelerated problems that were already occurring. Looking back at the events of that month, we can see that the following sequence of events led to the fall of the tsar.

### Strikes

During the winter, there had been a number of strikes protesting at the declining living standards of workers. This was nothing new: Russia had a history of industrial protests, which often led to clashes with police and soldiers sent by the government to end the strikes. The difference this time, was that the strikes occurred at a time when more people than ever were dissatisfied with the government of the tsar.

This increase in the number and size of strikes coincided with a new mood of protest that was already taking people out onto the streets of Petrograd.

## Timeline

### Key events of 1917

**January–February 1917** Mass protests in Petrograd

**27 February 1917** Army mutinies, Duma Committee set up

**April 1917** Lenin returns to Russia from exile

**July 1917** Kerensky takes control of Provisional Government; July Days

**24–25 October 1917** October Revolution

**23 February 1917** International Women's Day protests

**2 March 1917** Tsar Nicholas II abdicates; Duma Committee establishes Provisional Government

**June 1917** June Offensive

**August 1917** Kornilov Revolt

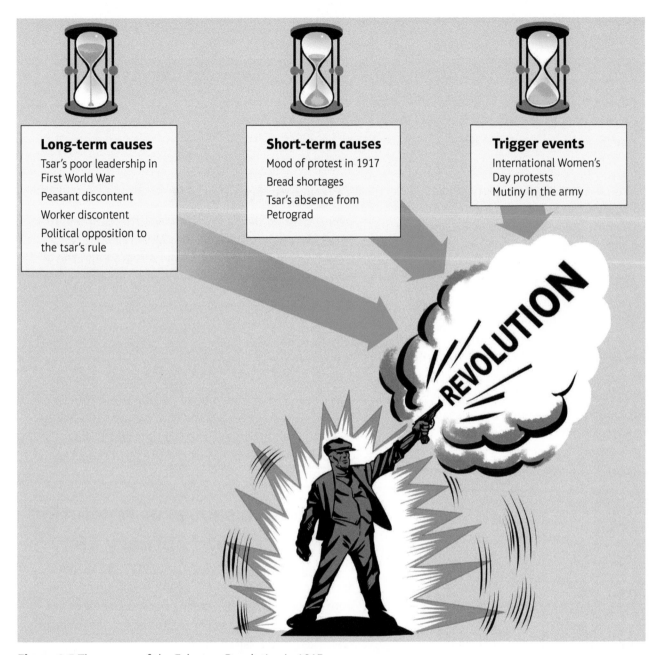

**Figure 1.5** The causes of the February Revolution in 1917.

On 18 February, another strike, demanding higher wages, started in the huge Putilov Steelworks. The mood of the strikers grew even more challenging when the owners of the steelworks declared a lockout – this meant they refused to let workers into their place of work and stopped paying them.

## Demonstrations

- On 9 January 1917, 150,000 workers had marched in memory of Bloody Sunday (1905) – when the tsar's soldiers had opened fire on a peaceful demonstration and had killed many.

- Another large demonstration – numbering about 80,000 – then took to the streets, on 14 February, in support of the duma and demanding that it influence the tsar.

- Just over a week later, the crowds of protesting workers were joined by the women protesters on International Women's Day.

- The mood on the streets was getting more dangerous – as it was also during that crucial week that the government announced that bread would soon be rationed.

- The demonstrations also increased in size because there was an unexpected improvement in the weather. The winter of 1916–1917 had been very cold, which had caused a lot of suffering to a civilian population that was already short of food and fuel as a result of the war. January and early February had been particularly cold – with heavy snow. Railway traffic had been disrupted, and Petrograd began to run out of flour for bread, and fuel. Then, in late February, the temperature rose in an unseasonal way. The mild weather encouraged more people to come out onto the streets of Petrograd to protest.

Nobody had planned this combination of events – but the large numbers of protesters soon became too much for the police to control. Over the course of two days (23–25 February) the size of the crowds rose to about 240,000, and there were clashes with the mounted police.

## The tsar's absence from Petrograd

The tsar's government was beginning to lose control of the capital city – but the tsar was miles away. Ever since he had taken over command of the military, he had spent most of his time at army headquarters. This was at Mogilev – which was around 780 kilometres from Petrograd. So unaware was he of the crisis that was building in Petrograd, that he actually left the city on 22 February to go to Mogilev. It was there that he finally received reports that the crowds were taking over the streets in his capital city. From Mogilev, the tsar issued orders to his police and army in Petrograd that the unrest in the city was to be stopped immediately. It was the evening of 25 February and – although the tsar did not know it – this order was about to cost him his throne.

# Mutiny in the army

On the afternoon of 26 February, soldiers opened fire on protesters and killed 40 of them. This caused soldiers in other regiments to begin questioning their orders. That evening, some soldiers of the Pavlovsky Guards Regiment refused to obey commands from their officers. This mutiny was quickly put down – but the next day things suddenly spiralled out of control. On 27 February, the same regiment that had shot the 40 demonstrators decided that it would no longer obey orders to use force against the crowds. Other regiments soon joined them –

they refused to obey orders, and began to give weapons to the crowds on the streets. Many of the soldiers involved were young conscripts, who had recently been called up to join the army, along with more experienced soldiers who were due to be sent back to the front and who were tired of the war.

Faced with the crowds of demonstrators on the streets, the police stopped trying to keep order. Worse than this, other soldiers sent into the city from the Petrograd garrison were refusing to fire on the crowd too, and were beginning to mix with the demonstrators. By the evening of 28 February, the military commander of Petrograd reported to the tsar, by telegraph, that revolutionary crowds were taking over all of the railway stations in the city and had seized all artillery supplies to the garrison. He couldn't use the telephone as control of the telephone exchange (from which land-lines were run) had been lost to the crowds. At this stage, the commander had few soldiers left who would obey the orders given to them by their officers.

### Activity ?

Design a protest poster, calling people out onto the streets of Petrograd in February 1917. On your poster include long-term reasons why change is needed, and reasons which explain why the winter of 1916–1917, and the running of the war, have finally caused you to want to overthrow the rule of Tsar Nicholas II.

### Source A

From the diary of M.M. Prishvin, recording events on 26 February 1917. Prishvin was a writer and a journalist. In February 1917, he was working as secretary to a member of the tsar's government.

```
No papers came out today, the 26th. The
whole city is full of troops. 'Who are
you guarding, then?' said some women to a
soldier. And it was obvious he didn't know
the answer: the enemy, his own people...

Right now all of the politics and state
policy can be expressed in the word 'bread'.
Just as at the beginning the whole life of
the state lay in the word 'war', now it's
'bread!... So a historian will call the first
part of the epoch [period of time] War and
the second Bread...'
```

## Source B

Mutinous soldiers on the streets of Petrograd in February 1917.

# The duma acts and confronts the tsar

As things began to fall apart in Petrograd, the members of the duma sent a petition to the tsar. This asked him to create a cabinet* that reflected the different parties represented in the duma. It also asked him to let the duma stay in session, as its time of meeting was about to come to an end. Despite all the problems that he was facing, the tsar refused both of these requests. The duma had thrown him a life-line – but he had refused to take hold of it.

One group of duma members refused to stop meeting: these were members of the Kadet Party and other liberals who hoped to reform Russia. They formed a group called the Duma Committee. Faced with this, the ministers of the tsar's government held one last meeting – which decided nothing – and then many of them left Petrograd.

## Key term

**Cabinet***

The senior members of a government, made up of ministers who run the various different departments of the government (for example, the army, treasury etc.) and take key decisions.

## Source C

From a report written by the tsar's secret police, the Okhrana, about events in Petrograd, on 26 February 1917. This was a secret report, not written for publication.

The movement broke out spontaneously [unplanned], without preparation and exclusively on the basis of the supply crisis. Inasmuch as the military units did not hinder the crowd and in individual cases even took steps to paralyze the actions of the police, the masses gained confidence that they could act with impunity [without being punished]. Now, after two days of unimpeded movement on the streets, when revolutionary circles have raised the slogans "Down with the war" and "Down with the government", the people have become convinced that the revolution has begun, that the masses are winning, that the authorities are powerless to suppress the movement by virtue of the fact that the military units are not on their side...

## Source D

From an account written by Mikhail Rodzianko, a conservative member and chair of the duma, one week after the army began to mutiny in Petrograd in February 1917. He believed that it was necessary for the tsar to abdicate and supported some reforms, but he was not in favour of revolutionary change.

Unexpectedly for all, there erupted a soldier mutiny such as I have never seen. These, of course, were not soldiers but muzhiki [peasants] taken directly from the plough who have found it useful now to make known their muzhik demands. In the crowd, all one could hear was "Land and Freedom", "Down with the Romanovs", "Down with the Officers".

## Activities ?

Look at Sources A, B, C and D.

1 For each source, write a sentence summing up what it says caused people to revolt in February 1917.

2 Which of these sources do you think is the most useful for explaining why the trouble on the streets started? Think about: (a) the strengths and weakness of each source as evidence, and (b) whether the source explains why the trouble started, or instead explains what it turned into later.

3 Which of these sources do you think is the most reliable for explaining why the protests became such a threat to the rule of the tsar? To do this, think about: who wrote the source; the kind of source it is; their point of view; how this affects the extent to which you can trust their opinion. Make a judgement and defend your decision in a paragraph of writing.

# Military commanders withdraw support for the tsar

Although the tsar seemed incapable of decisive action, there were those in the Army High Command who knew that something had to be done in response to the chaos in Petrograd. They had two options:

- **Option one** was a military solution: send in more soldiers and hope they could crush the growing revolt.
- **Option two** was a political solution: try to do a deal with the members of the duma and hope that they could put a stop to the disorder.

Since they feared that soldiers could no longer be trusted, they decided on option two.

Tsar Nicholas II was on his way back to Petrograd from Mogilev when he learned that the route to the city was blocked by mutinous troops. Instead, he was diverted to the city of Pskov, where he was met by high ranking army officers and members of the duma. They suggested that, in order to save Russia, the tsar should abdicate*. There was a short discussion and the tsar agreed. It was an astonishing anti-climax, and reveals how rapidly power had slipped out of the tsar's hands.

## Key term

**Abdicate***

When a monarch gives up their throne voluntarily.

At first Nicholas considered handing over power to his son: the Tsarevich Alexsei. However, Alexsei was a haemophiliac (suffering from a rare blood disorder in which blood does not clot when a person is cut or bruised). Concerned for the health of his son, Nicholas instead offered to hand over power to his own brother: Grand Duke Michael. Grand Duke Michael declined and Russia became a republic. Hundreds of years of tsarist rule had collapsed in a matter of days. This had not been planned by those who had persuaded the tsar to abdicate. As with so much in the February Revolution, things just ran out of control, and in directions that few could have predicted.

The members of the duma formed themselves into a 'Provisional* Government', which would govern Russia until a general election had taken place and a new government could be formed. Once this election had been held, the people's representatives, forming a

## Key term

**Provisional***

Temporary.

'Constituent Assembly', would then decide what kind of government Russia should have. The tsar was finally sent to join his family outside Petrograd, while the Provisional Government decided what to do with him.

# The role of the revolutionary parties in the February Revolution

The surprising thing about the February Revolution is that it owed little to the revolutionary political parties. The leaders of the Bolsheviks, and other political groups, were caught by surprise by the sudden collapse of the rule of the tsar. It was a revolution made on the streets, and the revolutionary parties had to run to catch up. Some of their leaders were in prison; some were in exile* in Siberia (a distant and inhospitable region of the Russian Empire); still others were in exile abroad. From his exile in Switzerland, Lenin could only follow the events back in Russia in the newspapers – with increasing frustration.

## Key term

**Exile***

Being sent away from your home area as a punishment; or going away voluntarily to avoid trouble at home.

In Petrograd, it was only as things started to get out of control that some members of revolutionary political groups helped organise protests – encouraging demonstrators and soldiers to rise up against the government of the tsar and overthrow it.

## Interpretation 1

From *The Russian Revolution 1899–1919*, by R. Pipes, published in 1992.

*It could be argued that the early disorders in Petrograd – and they had yet to occur in another city – were essentially a hunger riot... Whatever chance there was of containing the riots was destroyed by arrival in the evening of February 25 of a telegram from Nicholas... demanding that the disorders be suppressed by military force.*

## Interpretation 2

From *Lenin, Stalin and Hitler*, by R. Gellately, published in 2007.

*By the beginning of 1917, widespread discontent over the ghastly sacrifices of the war, food shortages, and high prices led to bitter strikes and hostile demonstrations.*

*The pent-up resentment and grievances were ignited by a demonstration in the capital on 23 February, when a peaceful march for women's rights was joined by striking workers. Cries rang out for bread and people exclaimed, "Down with the tsar!"*

*Instead of charging the crowds, tens of thousands of peasant soldiers, their mentality shaped by decades of grievances against the system, went over to the people.*

## Exam-style questions, Section B

- Study Interpretations 1 and 2, which give different views about the causes of the February Revolution of 1917. What is the main difference between these views? Explain your answer, using details from both interpretations. **4 marks**

- How far do you agree with Interpretation 2 about the causes of the February Revolution of 1917? Explain your answer, using both interpretations and your knowledge of the historical context. **20 marks**

## Exam tip

- For question 1, identify a clear point of difference and back up your answer from the source.

- With a 'How far…' question, it is a good idea to first say what you agree with and why, and then what you disagree with and why. Then conclude with deciding whether you mostly agree or disagree.

## Summary

- In February 1917, 'trigger causes' led to the downfall of the tsar.
- These had such a powerful effect because they were added to a rising tide of discontent with the war.
- The 'trigger causes' were added to short-term and long-term reasons why people wanted change.
- The absence of the tsar from Petrograd meant that these challenges got out of control without him fully understanding the threat he was facing.
- The decision of the tsar to ignore the duma, and rely on force, caused the unrest to explode into revolution.
- The political parties played little part in the February Revolution of 1917.
- The Revolution of February 1917 was unplanned, and nobody was sure exactly what it would lead to in Russia.

## Checkpoint

### Strengthen

**S1** Explain the problems the war was causing Russia by February 1917.

**S2** Explain what a 'trigger cause' is, and say what you think the most important one was in February 1917.

**S3** Why were the February 1917 demonstrations so difficult for the police to control?

### Challenge

**C1** In your own words, explain the biggest mistake made by the tsar in February 1917.

**C2** Could revolution have been avoided in February 1917?

How confident do you feel about your answers to these questions? If you are not sure you answered them well, look again at Interpretations 1 and 2 and discuss these challenges in small groups.

# 1.3 The Provisional Government

## What was the Provisional Government?

In February 1917, the rule of Tsar Nicholas II came to an end and Russia became a republic. From February until October, the government of Russia was the Provisional Government. Some moderate Russians hoped that this new form of government would lead the way to Russia becoming a democracy. Yet, by the autumn, these hopes were in ruins – and a very different set of rulers was installed in Petrograd. As a result of these events, Russia began 1917 as a tsarist monarchy, and ended 1917 on its way to becoming a communist dictatorship under the control of the Bolsheviks. How this occurred is one of the most important questions of 20th century history.

## Setting up the Provisional Government

Towards the end of February 1917, it was becoming clear that the tsar was not going to co-operate with the members of the duma in changing Russia into a constitutional monarchy*. Instead he ordered the duma to stop meeting and not to re-assemble until April. Eventually, the leading members of the duma decided to defy this order and set up the 'Duma Committee' to work for political change. The chairman was Mikhail Rodzianko (see Section 1.2, Source D).

### Key term

**Constitutional monarchy***

Rule by a king or queen whose powers are limited by a parliament.

The decision of the duma to act was accelerated by the fact that revolutionary groups were already planning to set up their own soviet*.

### Key term

**Soviet***

A committee of elected members, representing workers, soldiers and peasants. There had been a Petrograd Soviet following a failed revolution in 1905. The memory of it was very strong – and left wing groups felt that it was the kind of government that would best represent the ordinary people of Russia.

Across the city, factory workers, and mutinous army and naval units, elected representatives to the new Petrograd Soviet. The Duma Committee was holding its meetings in the Tauride Palace; and Rodzianko gave two Menshevik (see page 13) members of the Duma Committee permission to hold Petrograd Soviet meetings there too. By the evening of 27 February, both the Duma Committee and the 'provisional executive committee of the Petrograd Soviet' were meeting at the palace. The first was moderate, and the second far more revolutionary; but, to start with, they were united by their fear of being crushed by the tsar.

On 2 March, following the abdication of the tsar, the Duma Committee formally established the Provisional Government. It was under the leadership of Prince Lvov and other liberal politicians. Their first acts were to:

- release political and religious prisoners
- promise full democratic freedom
- end the death penalty
- take over land belonging to the tsar
- take local government, across Russia, out of the hands of tsarist officials, and transfer power to local councils (called, in Russian, zemstvos).

The Provisional Government was also determined to carry on with the war. The reasons being: they needed the support of their Western allies, Britain and France; they needed the support of the army generals; and there had been no popular demand for Russia to sign a separate peace treaty with its enemies – Germany and Austria-Hungary. There was also a feeling that it was the right thing to do – as Russia had suffered so much in the war, it should fight on to achieve victory.

## The problems faced by the Provisional Government

However, things were already getting chaotic – as across Russia, just as in Petrograd, workers and soldiers were electing soviets. The question was: who was going to be in charge of Russia? Was it the Provisional Government, or the Petrograd Soviet and the network of local soviets? Russia was heading into a system known to historians as the period of 'Dual Control'. There were, in effect, two governments in Russia: the Provisional Government and the network of soviets that looked towards the Petrograd Soviet.

- The Petrograd Soviet controlled the railway system and the postal and telegraph service – because these were industries in which workers supported the soviet. This caused major problems for the Provisional Government, as these key areas were out of its control.
- Ordinary members of army units and naval ships took over control of the units and ships, and elected members to the Petrograd Soviet. Some officers were murdered.
- The Petrograd Soviet set up groups to organise food supplies – yet another responsibility of the government that it had lost to the soviet. The Petrograd Soviet even had its own newspaper to spread its ideas: this was called Izvestya (Russian for 'News').

In March, something called the 'Central Executive Committee' was set up, which claimed to represent all of the workers' and soldiers' soviets that had sprung up over Russia.

On top of all this, Russia was still in the middle of the worst war in European history; and the Provisional Government found itself in charge of the country at this incredibly difficult time.

## The role of Kerensky

Alexander Kerensky was a lawyer and a moderate socialist. He was both a member of the Provisional Government and a member of the Petrograd Soviet. Within the Provisional Government, he was first the Minister of Justice and then, in May 1917, he became Minister of War.

In July 1917, after the failure of the June Offensive (see page 26), Kerensky became the Minister-Chairman (leader) of the Provisional Government, in place of Prince Lvov. Kerensky held this post until the Provisional Government was overthrown by the Bolsheviks in October 1917.

He was a skilful speaker, but he made some crucial mistakes: he continued with the war – angering many ordinary soldiers while, at the same time, losing support of army officers by reducing their authority; his actions to weaken old ruling groups lost him the support of conservatives; and he failed to take tough action against the Bolsheviks – who would eventually overthrow him.

# The weaknesses and failures of the Provisional Government

The Provisional Government lacked decisive leadership. Even when it did gain a more determined leader – in Kerensky – its other weaknesses and failures contributed to its eventual collapse.

## Lack of control over the military

On 1 March, the soldiers of the Petrograd garrison published 'Order Number 1'. It said that the army and navy would only obey orders from the Provisional Government if they were also approved by the Petrograd Soviet. The soviet adopted the order – even though they weren't originally involved in making it. This hugely undermined the authority of the Provisional Government. In the event of a disagreement, it would now be the Petrograd Soviet that had the final say on military matters.

Order Number 1 also said that regiments would now take responsibility for discipline in the military; and this would be done by councils of ordinary soldiers – not by officers under the authority of the Provisional Government. Again this greatly weakened the Provisional Government's position.

## Source A

From 'Order Number 1' published by the Petrograd garrison on 1 March 1917 and later by the Petrograd Soviet.

```
1. In all companies, battalions, regiments...
and on the vessels of the navy, committees
of elected representatives from the lower
ranks of the above-mentioned military units
shall be chosen...

2. The orders of the military commission of
the State duma shall be executed [carried
out] only in such cases as they do not
conflict with the orders and resolutions of
the Soviet of Workers' and Soldiers' Deputies
[Petrograd Soviet].

7. Also, the addressing of the officers with
the titles "Your Excellency", "Your Honour",
and the like, is abolished, and these titles
are replaced by "Mr General", "Mr Colonel"
and so forth.
```

## Source B

From a letter written in March 1917 by the Provisional Government's War Minister Guchkov, to the commander of the army.

```
The Provisional Government does not possess
any real power; and its directives are
carried out only to the extent that it is
permitted by the Soviet of Workers' and
Soldiers' Deputies... since the troops, the
railroads, the post and telegraph are all
in its hands. One can say flatly that the
Provisional Government exists only so long
as it is permitted by the Soviet.
```

## Failure to hold a general election

The Provisional Government lacked legitimacy. In other words, people in general did not feel that it had authority and should be obeyed. This is because the duma from which it was formed had originally been elected (in 1912) under the tsarist system, which only gave the vote to a small percentage of people. When the Provisional Government was formed in 1917, it was little more than a group of well-meaning people. They did not represent the wider population, and yet they claimed authority over all of Russia. Compared to the direct elections of workers, soldiers and peasants to the soviets, the Provisional Government did not look very representative – so it is unsurprising that it had little authority.

The Provisional Government genuinely intended to hold a general election; but there were so many problems facing Russia in the spring and summer of 1917 – including the war – and organising an election would have been such an enormous task, that they put it off until later in the year. However, delaying the election proved to be a big mistake – as it allowed people to say the government lacked popular support.

## Failure to meet peasant demands

The one thing that almost all peasants wanted was more land. After that, most peasants just wanted to be left alone to get on with their lives. In Russia, there was a history of occasional and violent uprisings of peasants against their landlords – but not of an organised political plan for changing Russia. The SRs were supported by many peasants, and hoped to create a socialist Russia based on their support; but most peasants had little interest in the long term plans of the SRs. The relationship between the SRs and the peasants has been described by one historian as a 'one-sided love affair'.

One way of keeping the peasants happy might have been to let them seize the land of the great landowners – and even their wealthier peasant neighbours. However, the Provisional Government was reluctant to do this, for three main reasons:

- Firstly, it thought it should wait until after a general election before allowing huge changes.
- Secondly, it feared that if land was redistributed among the peasants then huge numbers of soldiers fighting at the front would desert and return home in order not to miss out. After all, most of those fighting in the Russian army and navy were peasants who had been conscripted to fight.
- Thirdly, the Provisional Government was afraid of Russia simply falling apart in disorganised violence and disorder.

This reluctance to act was also to prove a major mistake. Many peasants just got on with seizing land anyway, and they resented soldiers sent by the Provisional Government to stop them. Later, they would give support (even if it was half-hearted) to any political party which promised to let them take land. As we shall see, the Bolsheviks – under Lenin – were quick to make the most of this.

## Continuing to fight the war: the June Offensive

Continuing to fight the war was unpopular. The Petrograd Soviet supported the war only if it was defending Russian territory: they thought there should be no advances, and no plans to seize enemy territory (in the unlikely event of the Russian army being in a position to take any). Among ordinary members of the soviet, the troops, the workers, and the general population, the matter was simple: end the war and bring the soldiers home.

However, in June 1917, while Kerensky was still War Minister, the Provisional Government ordered a new attack. The Russian army, under the command of General Brusilov, attacked the Austrian and German armies in Galicia (southern Poland). The attack was a disaster: Russian soldiers refused to advance and there were 200,000 Russian casualties. The army was driven backwards as the Germans advanced into Ukraine (at that time ruled by Russia).

In the aftermath of the June Offensive, Kerensky took over leadership of the Provisional Government from Prince Lvov.

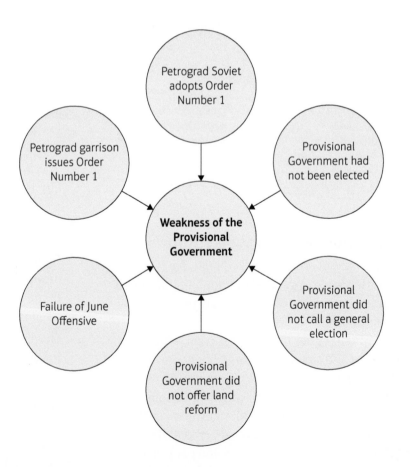

**Figure 1.6**: Factors contributing to the weakness of the Provisional Government.

---

**Activities** ?

1 Copy the spidergram (Figure 1.6) and colour-code it for a) mistakes the Provisional Government made, b) actions of the soviets, c) other factors.

2 'The Provisional Government had only itself to blame for the fact that it lost most of its support by the end of the June Offensive in 1917'. How far do you agree with this statement? First think about problems that the Provisional Government created through its own actions. Then think about problems that it had no control over. Finally, make a judgement about where you think the main blame lay by the summer of 1917.

---

# The Kornilov Revolt

Support for the Provisional Government had never been strong. By August 1917 it was draining away. Soldiers were angry about the disastrous June Offensive. Many workers were in favour of the Petrograd Soviet taking power because it would give them more influence. Peasants were seizing land. Russia was falling apart. It was at this point that General Kornilov attempted to seize power.

## Who was General Kornilov and what were his aims?

General Kornilov had recently been made Commander-in-Chief of the Russian army by Kerensky, with orders to restore discipline in the army. Kornilov's aims in leading a revolt seem to have been:

- to create a strong government
- to defeat the revolutionary groups in Petrograd.

He may have thought that Kerensky supported his revolt, but whether or not this is true is unclear. Kerensky seems to have been aware of Kornilov's plans, but did not act until the revolt was actually under way.

## Why did the Kornilov Revolt fail?

In late August, Kornilov ordered troops to Petrograd to restore order. His action failed because: firstly, soldiers were no longer following orders; and, secondly, Petrograd workers acted to defend their revolution. Printers refused to print newspapers that expressed support for Kornilov; railway workers disrupted the trains carrying soldiers; and steelworkers met the trains and persuaded soldiers to desert.

## The impact of the Kornilov Revolt on the Provisional Government

The Kornilov Revolt further weakened Kerensky and the Provisional Government in a number of ways:

- Kerensky was accused of sympathising with Kornilov and assisting him.
- Distrust between soldiers and officers increased.
- There was a surge of support for the Bolsheviks amongst workers and soldiers. The Bolsheviks were seen as the only group prepared to defend the Petrograd Soviet from the threat of Kornilov. The Bolsheviks were also the only party that had never supported the Provisional Government and that was prepared to use force to increase workers' power.
- Workers formed themselves into armed units called 'Red Guards' to protect the Petrograd Soviet from Kornilov's troops. Most of the men in these groups were Bolsheviks or Bolshevik supporters. This gave the Bolsheviks a huge military advantage over the Provisional Government, which struggled to find soldiers that it could rely on to obey its orders.

At the same time, the German army was advancing further into Russian territory. By September 1917, things did not look good for Kerensky and the Provisional Government. In October, the situation facing them would become even worse (see Section 1.4).

### Extend your knowledge

**Kornilov after the Bolshevik Revolution**

When General Kornilov's revolt failed he was put into prison. He later escaped and led an army against the new Bolshevik government (see Section 1.4). His troops had a reputation for great brutality. Again the revolt failed. Kornilov was eventually killed by an exploding artillery shell in April 1918. His body was dug up and burnt on a village rubbish dump by victorious Bolsheviks.

### Interpretation 1

From *The Bolshevik Revolution: A Social History of the Russian Revolution*, by M. Ferro, published in 1985.

'Between February and October, the tide of Revolution became a flood, and we could not halt or direct it,' said Kerensky, and it applied to the leaders... of all the parties. They had expected to lead the movement, to hasten or to retard [slow down] it; unless they could at least follow it, they would be swept away. They were aware of their own powerlessness, but they did not understand it. They had worked for the Revolution but, now that it had broken out, the masses [ordinary people] behaved in ways they had not foreseen or planned.

## Source C

A Red Guard unit, photographed in 1917.

### Exam-style question, Section A

How useful are Sources A and B for an enquiry into the weaknesses of the Provisional Government in 1917?

Explain your answer, using Sources A and B, and your own knowledge of the historical context.　**8 marks**

### Exam tip

Look at what each Source suggests about the weaknesses of the Provisional Government. Compare this with what you know about problems it faced. Decide how you could use what each source tells you in order to carry out the enquiry.

## Summary

- The Provisional Government faced many problems when it came to power.
- Its power was challenged by the Petrograd Soviet and by Order Number 1.
- It added to its problems by not holding a general election, not giving land to peasants, by continuing with the war and by not controlling General Kornilov.

## Checkpoint

### Strengthen

**S1** List three problems facing the Provisional Government after it took power.

**S2** Decide which of these problems most seriously weakened it.

### Challenge

**C1** How was the Provisional Government weakened by problems in these areas: political (ideas about running the country); social (standards of living and how society was organised); and military (to do with the war)?

**C2** Why is it difficult for modern historians to decide on one overall reason for the weakness of the Provisional Government?

How confident do you feel about your answers to these questions? For C2, think about how many different problems the Provisional Government faced, and how this makes it hard to decide on a main cause.

# 1.4 The Bolshevik Revolution

## The Bolsheviks and Lenin

In February 1917, nobody would have imagined that the extreme left wing group, known as the Bolsheviks, would have seized power in Russia by the end of the year. This outcome was surprising because:

- they were just one of several revolutionary groups
- they had a fairly small number of supporters, and only 23,000 members (the total population of Russia at this time was 145 million); in early 1917, their main rivals – the Mensheviks – outnumbered them
- many important Bolshevik figures were in exile – Lenin, their overall leader, was in Switzerland
- like most revolutionary groups, the Bolsheviks had played next to no part in the February Revolution.

In early 1917, the Bolsheviks did not look like they could become the ruling political party in Russia. But the following months brought dramatic changes.

## Lenin's return

When the February Revolution occurred, Lenin was in exile in Zurich, Switzerland. He was desperate to get back to Russia. In the end it was the Russian enemy – the Germans – who made this possible. They were keen to cause as much upheaval in Russia as possible, in the hope that the Russians would pull out of the war. The German government hated Bolshevik political views, but felt that if Lenin returned to Russia it would cause trouble for the Provisional Government. They were correct.

The Germans arranged for Lenin, his wife Krupskaya, and a small group of followers to cross Germany in a sealed train. Nobody was allowed to get on or off it. From Germany, Lenin travelled through neutral Sweden, and then Finland, to arrive by train at Petrograd's Finland Station on 3 April. There he was met by members of the Bolshevik leadership and their supporters.

### Extend your knowledge

**Lenin as leader**

Lenin had a ruthless personality. He lived for politics and had followers rather than friends. He was highly intelligent and skilled at communicating complex ideas in accessible ways – but he was always certain that he was right. Although fanatical and determined, he was not vain or corrupt. He had a reputation as a 'splitter': he would find something to fall out with an opponent over, then leave with anyone who would back him. He treated opponents with contempt and ridicule. He was uncompromising and confrontational. Although these personality characteristics were unattractive in an individual – and encouraged cold brutality once he was in power – they were advantages in the chaos of Russia in 1917.

### The 'April Theses'

When Lenin returned to Petrograd he was not at all pleased with the state of the Bolshevik Party. Two members of the Bolshevik leadership already in Petrograd – Kamenev and Stalin – were supporting the Provisional Government – as they thought that Russia was not yet ready for a further revolution. They were even considering reuniting with their old rivals, the Mensheviks, who had a lot more members.

As soon as Lenin arrived at the Finland Station he rejected any idea of co-operation with the Provisional Government. Instead, he argued that the Bolsheviks should prepare to seize power from the Provisional Government and create what he described as a 'workers' revolution'.

Later, communist films and artwork would present Lenin's return as a triumph, with enthusiastic crowds of workers cheering his call for a Bolshevik uprising.

In 1926, the communist government of Russia had a statue put up outside the Finland Station to remind people of Lenin's triumphant return.

## Source A

Painted in the 1930s, during the period of communist government in Russia, this shows Lenin speaking to a huge crowd of supporters at the Finland Station. Stalin, who ruled Russia after Lenin, is shown standing just behind him when, in reality, he was not even there.

But, the reality in April 1917 was a little different. Many of the Bolshevik leaders were shocked at what Lenin said. They felt Lenin was out of touch with what was going on in Russia. They also felt that he was ignoring one of their key communist beliefs: that a workers' revolution could only happen in an advanced industrial country, and after capitalists had ruled a country for some time. In Russia, most people were still peasants; and industrial growth was well behind that of Germany, France, Britain and the USA. Some soldiers even muttered that they should stick their bayonets into Lenin!

Finally, though, Lenin had his way, and argued the other Bolsheviks round to his way of thinking. He was helped in this by new members who were joining the Bolsheviks. Many were workers, who were not interested in being cautious or waiting to take power. Instead, they wanted immediate action. By April, the membership of the Bolsheviks had risen to 75,000.

Lenin summed up what he wanted in his 'April Theses'. In a list of ten demands, he called for:

- rejection of the Provisional Government
- all power to pass to the soviets
- workers to enjoy the wealth of Russia
- an end to the war
- taking over of land owned by rich landowners.

In doing this, Lenin was aiming to increase support for the Bolsheviks among Russian workers, soldiers and peasants. His demands soon began to be summarised in the easily understood slogan: 'Bread, Peace, Land'.

## Source B

Points from Lenin's April Theses, 1917.

```
No support for the Provisional Government;
the utter falsity of all its promises should
be made clear...

The masses must be made to see that the
Soviets of Worker's Deputies are the only
possible form of revolutionary government...

Not a parliamentary republic... but a
republic of Soviets of Workers, Agricultural
Labourers and Peasants' Deputies throughout
the country, from top to bottom...

Abolition of the police, the army and the
bureaucracy [government officials]...

Confiscation of all landed estates...

Nationalization [making private property
into state-owned property] of all lands in
the country...
```

## Activities ?

1. Write a short report as if you were a German agent in Switzerland advising your government to arrange Lenin's return to Russia. Explain who Lenin is, what he is like, and why it would be useful to Germany to get him back into Russia.

2. Now write a short diary extract as if you were a Bolshevik who met Lenin at the Finland Station on 3 April 1917. What aspects of his speech might you be less impressed by?

3. Source A is not an accurate representation of what Lenin's return was really like. So why is it still useful to historians studying the history of Russia? Discuss with a partner.

## Growing support for the Bolsheviks

Support for the Bolsheviks – from workers and the armed forces – gradually increased throughout the early summer of 1917.

In June, an All-Russian Congress of Soviets met in Petrograd. This was an attempt to set up a group to represent the many soviets that had sprung up across Russia. There were just over 800 representatives at the meeting. Of these, 285 were SRs, 248 were Mensheviks and only 105 were Bolsheviks. This is a reminder that support for the Bolsheviks was limited at first, and the SRs were much more popular, especially with peasants. At the congress, Lenin announced there was a party present that was ready to take control of the government – he meant the Bolsheviks. Most of those present thought his claim was absurd, and rejected it.

Others, however, were listening. Active work by Bolsheviks – in factories, army units, and on ships of the Baltic fleet at Kronstadt – began to convince many that if they backed Lenin, they could finally have a say in how Russia would be run and how its wealth would be shared. The Bolsheviks were careful to say that they were doing this on behalf of the soviets. In addition, many ordinary workers, soldiers and sailors were even more radical than many of the leaders of the revolutionary parties. The suffering and turmoil of the war, and then the end of tsarism, had changed many people in Russia. Bolshevik ambitions fitted well with the new mood. It was beginning to look as if an alternative kind of government – different to the Provisional Government – might really be set up in Russia.

The Bolsheviks were also helped by money secretly provided by Germany. With this assistance, they set up 41 newspapers across Russia by June. In the same month, the All-Russian Congress of Soviets organised a demonstration. Many were surprised to find that most of the banners workers carried at the demonstration had Bolshevik slogans on them. People had not yet realised how popular the Bolsheviks had become. In the factories, the armed workers militias* – known as the Red Guards – becoming increasingly sympathetic to the

### Key term

**Militia***

Armed civilian group.

Bolsheviks. Support for the Bolsheviks grew further after the Kornilov Revolt (see page 27). By July there were about 10,000 Red Guards in Petrograd.

## The 'July Days'

In July 1917 – in protest against the Provisional Government's 'June Offensive' – army units in Petrograd refused to go to the front. They were supported by a large number of Petrograd factory workers, and also by sailors at the Kronstadt naval base, about 30 kilometres from Petrograd in the Gulf of Finland. On 3 July, they marched on the Tauride Palace in Petrograd and demanded that the Petrograd Soviet take power. Workers, soldiers and sailors were turning out to be more revolutionary than the members of the soviet themselves.

This was what the Bolsheviks wanted, but they don't seem to have organised it. Lenin was not in Petrograd at the time, and the Bolshevik Central Committee was divided over what to do. When they said the demonstration should continue, it was probably only because they feared disappointing the crowds if they said anything else.

However, the Bolsheviks were blamed for organising the 'July Days'. The Provisional Government brought soldiers in from the front to defend itself, and denounced the Bolsheviks as German spies. Lenin went into hiding and ended up back in Finland. Leading Bolsheviks were arrested, including Kamenev and Trotsky, who had recently left the Mensheviks to join the Bolsheviks.

The Bolsheviks were not completely crushed, and even managed to hold a party congress soon after the July Days – but it looked as if Kerensky had seen off the Bolshevik threat.

However, no sooner had this happened, than he faced the threat from the Kornilov Revolt, which further weakened him and increased opposition to the Provisional Government.

### Activity ?

Design a leaflet that might have been handed out on the streets of Petrograd in July 1917, calling on workers to oppose the Provisional Government. What reasons would it give? Use Source B and other information from this section (1.4) to help you decide what to include.

# The build-up to revolution

By September 1917, the Provisional Government was in deep trouble. The Kornilov Revolt had severely weakened it. Support for the Bolsheviks was rising in the factories, in the army and navy, and among the workers' Red Guards. Discipline in the army had finally collapsed. Across Russia, peasants were seizing land and resented any attempt by the Provisional Government to stop them. So-called 'factory committees' of workers controlled most factories – and many of the workers were Bolsheviks. Rumours were spreading that Kerensky would abandon Petrograd to the advancing German army. The time seemed ripe for the Bolsheviks to seize power. On 31 August, the Bolsheviks gained a majority in the Petrograd Soviet; and on 5 September they achieved the same position in Moscow.

## The role of Lenin

Lenin was skilful in appealing to the mood of the people. While he was in hiding in Finland, after the 'July Days', he wrote a booklet called *State and Revolution*, in which he said, that once a revolution had succeeded, there would be a brief time (called 'the dictatorship of the Proletariat') in which the old classes and rulers would be swept away. Soon after that, there would be a classless society and the state would wither away.

This appealed to many ordinary Russians, who were tired of being controlled. It promised freedom – but said very little about the Bolshevik Party. It sounded as if the Bolsheviks were going to do all this on behalf of the soviets, who would then rule Russia as it headed into a time of freedom and prosperity for ordinary people. In the end, once the Bolsheviks were in power, Russia ended up with something rather different.

From exile in Finland, Lenin sent messages back to Petrograd during September – demanding action. By this time, the Bolsheviks had their headquarters in the Smolny Institute in Petrograd, which had once been a private girls' school. Other Bolsheviks were not convinced that they could successfully seize power and make a communist state work in such an under-developed country. However, Lenin was convinced that a revolution in Russia would ignite others across Europe – particularly in Germany – this would help the revolution in Russia survive.

On 10 October, Lenin secretly returned to Petrograd. At a stormy meeting of 12 senior Bolsheviks, Lenin was opposed by two leading Bolsheviks – Kamenev and Zinoviev – but finally argued a majority round to his way of thinking.

## The role of Trotsky

Lenin wanted the Red Guards to seize power immediately. However, he was still spending much of his time in Finland, so had to leave the detailed planning to former Menshevik, Trotsky. Trotsky thought it would be better to seize power just before the second All-Russian Congress of Soviets met later in October. The Congress would then be forced to accept what had been done.

Trotsky had been elected the chairman of the Petrograd Soviet. This gave him an opportunity to use its Military Revolutionary Committee (MRC) to seize power. The committee had been set up to defend Petrograd from a German attack, and was largely Bolshevik in its membership. By 23 October, the MRC had control over all soldiers in Petrograd, including those in the powerful Peter-Paul Fortress. The Bolsheviks were now in a position to make their move. By the time that Lenin returned to Petrograd once more – on the night of 24–25 October – he found, to his relief, that the revolution had already started.

## Interpretation 1

From *History of the USSR* by Y. Kukushkin, published in the USSR in 1981.

*The Bolshevik party was waging a determined struggle to win over the masses. The struggle was headed by Lenin who led and guided the Party's Central Committee, and the editorial board of the Party's newspaper Pravda… He frequently addressed mass rallies and meetings. Lenin's appearance on the platform invariably triggered off the acclamations and enthusiasm of the audience. Lenin's speeches, noted for their profound content and brilliant delivery, inspired the workers and soldiers to a determined struggle.*

Later propaganda made Lenin the hero of the revolution. Source C shows him directing troops at the Smolny Palace, even though it was Trotsky who was actually in charge. However, although it was Trotsky who organised the seizure of power, this would not have been possible if Lenin had not persuaded the Bolshevik leadership that it was right to take power. Without Lenin the revolution would not have happened.

## Source C

A 1930s painting, by the Russian artist Mikhail Sokolov, showing Lenin organising the Red Guards at the Smolny Institute.

## Interpretation 2

From *Lenin* by R. Service, published in 2000.

*Films were made of the October Revolution, novels written, songs sung and even ballets danced. In practically all of them a misleading image of Lenin was disseminated. There he is, with his fist raised, mouth tensed and a bearded chin. In fact, on that historic day of 25 October 1917 he spoke only briefly. He was not the Revolution's great orator... Contrary to conventional accounts, then, Lenin's importance was not as a speaker in the Congress hall but rather as a strategist and inspirer behind the scenes — and in this role his contribution to the Revolution's success was crucial.*

## The Bolshevik Revolution: the seizure of power

On the same night that Lenin returned to Petrograd (24–25 October) Red Guards occupied key positions in the city. As the second All-Russian Congress of Soviets gathered – on the afternoon of 25 October – fighting was still going on across the city. Mensheviks and SRs protested that the Bolsheviks were seizing power

### Activities ?

1   Look at Interpretations 1 and 2. For each one, write a sentence summarising its view of the importance of Lenin in making the October Revolution happen.

2   How far do you agree with Interpretation 2 on Lenin's role in organising the October revolution? Use the interpretation and your own knowledge.

3   Look at Source C. How accurate is this representation of the events of October 1917? Look at the details of the source and compare it with what you know.

without the agreement of the other revolutionary groups. They were ignored – and so walked out of the congress in protest.

On the evening of 25 October, Red Guards and sailors from Kronstadt advanced on the old tsarist Winter Palace – where the Provisional Government had its headquarters. Their attack was signalled by blank shots fired from a naval vessel, the cruiser Aurora, anchored nearby.

The palace was defended by officer cadets and a women's battalion – Kerensky could not persuade more experienced troops to support him anymore. Earlier that day he had driven round the city, in a car borrowed from the American Embassy, trying – and failing – to find soldiers to fight for him and the Provisional Government.

The palace fell to the Bolsheviks with hardly a fight. Red Guards climbed in through the windows until they outnumbered the inexperienced defenders. Some ministers of the Provisional Government were arrested, but Kerensky escaped and eventually fled from Russia.

By the early hours of 26 October, it was all over. It was declared at the Congress of Soviets that the Bolsheviks had taken power across Russia. In fact, the fighting went on for several days in Moscow, and it would be some time before news of what was going on in Petrograd spread to the rest of the country.

## Extend your knowledge

### The Winter Palace on film

In 1928, the Bolsheviks released a film of the storming of the Winter Palace. Called 'October' it was directed by the famous Russian film directors, Aleksandrov and Eisenstein. Its dramatic scenes of gunfire, explosions and smoke make the capture seem like a great battle. Finally the palace falls to the Red Guards, who pour through the gates. It later became a joke in the Russian film industry that more people were shot (accidentally) while making the film in 1928 than in the actual storming of the Winter Palace in 1917.

## Source D

A still from the film 'October', released in 1928 in Russia, showing huge numbers of Red Guards storming the Winter Palace.

## THINKING HISTORICALLY    Interpretations (4a)

### The weight of evidence

Historian's interpretations are not simply their opinions: interpretations are theories. In order for theories to be strong, they need to be backed up with convincing evidence. When you evaluate an interpretation, you should consider how strong the evidence is for the conclusions it comes to.

Work in pairs. Look at Source C and Conclusions 1-3 below, then answer the questions.

### Conclusion 1

Lenin played a major role in October 1917, as is reflected in his active involvement in organising the Red Guards, who are carefully listening to his instructions.

### Conclusion 2

Bolshevik preparations for the seizure of power in October 1917 ensured that they were ready to take power and had the support of the workers. These worker Red Guards are armed and ready to use force to support the revolution.

### Conclusion 3

The leadership of Lenin in 1917 was important but later Soviet paintings overplayed his role. In this painting there is no depiction of Trotsky, even though it was Trotsky who actually organised the seizure of power.

1   Write out each conclusion and then use highlighter pens to colour code them. Use one colour for 'evidence', another colour for 'conclusions' and a third for language that shows 'reasoning' (e.g. "therefore", "so").

2   How do the conclusions differ in terms of the way that the evidence is used?

3   Put the conclusions in ranking order from the best to the worst. Explain your choice.

4   Consider what you know about Lenin's role. For each conclusion, add any extra evidence you can think of that supports that conclusion.

5   Rank the conclusions again. Does the evidence you have added change which you think is the best?

6   Using evidence from the interpretation, and your own knowledge, write your own conclusion about the importance of Lenin in the success of the October Revolution. Remember to back up all your points by reasoning about the evidence.

# Reasons for Bolshevik success

The Provisional Government lacked support and made itself even more unpopular by continuing the war. The Kornilov Revolt further weakened it.

The Bolsheviks were not associated with support for the Provisional Government. Lenin provided strong leadership, and Trotsky was a skilled organiser. They also had financial help from the German government.

Slogans such as 'Bread, Peace, Land' summed up the popular mood and were easily understood. These promises appealed to workers, soldiers and peasants.

The Bolsheviks were more in tune with the radical demands of workers, soldiers and peasants in 1917 than the other revolutionary parties.

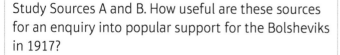

## Exam-style question, Section B

Study Sources A and B. How useful are these sources for an enquiry into popular support for the Bolsheviks in 1917?

Explain your answer, using Sources A and B, and your knowledge of the historical context. **8 marks**

## Exam tip

Evaluate the strengths and weaknesses of Sources A and B as evidence for an historian assessing what happened in 1917, and how much support the Bolsheviks had. Compare what the sources say with what you know about the situation in 1917.

## Summary

- Lenin made it clear that the Bolsheviks should not support the Provisional Government. Instead, they should work towards overthrowing it on behalf of the soviets.
- Support for the Bolsheviks increased among workers and soldiers during 1917.
- The actual organisation of the 'October Revolution' was left to Trotsky.

## Checkpoint

### Strengthen

**S1** How did Lenin's attitude towards the Provisional Government differ from other Bolsheviks?

**S2** Why did support for the Bolsheviks increase over the summer of 1917?

**S3** Why did the Mensheviks and SRs disapprove of the Bolshevik uprising in October 1917?

### Challenge

**C1** Why did Lenin claim that the October Revolution was on behalf of the soviets?

**C2** Who was more important in making the October Revolution happen: Lenin or Trotsky?

**C3** The Bolsheviks were able to take power because of economic, political and military factors. In your own words, explain how these combined to enable the Bolsheviks to seize power.

How confident do you feel about your answers to these questions? If you are not confident about your answer to C3, create a spidergram showing causes of the failure of the Provisional Government, and causes of the success of the Bolsheviks; colour code it for economic, political, and military causes; then decide how the different causes led to the October Revolution.

# Recap: The revolutions of 1917

## Recall quiz

1. What was the name of the ruler of Russia in 1914?
2. Which political party had a lot of support from peasants?
3. Who was the leader of the Bolsheviks?
4. What is the Russian word for a parliament?
5. What special day of marches led to the outbreak of the February Revolution?
6. Why was it a mistake for the tsar to become commander-in-chief of the army?
7. What is the Russian word for a revolutionary council of workers, soldiers and peasants?
8. What was the title of Lenin's publication produced when he first returned to Russia?
9. Who led a military revolt against the Provisional Government in August 1917?
10. Who organised the Bolshevik October Revolution?

## Activity ?

Historians have different opinions (interpretations) about what led to the October Revolution of 1917. This is because the evidence is complicated, and there were lots of different things that led to it. Look at each one of these possible interpretations. For each one, write a short paragraph which explains what evidence might support this interpretation.

*'It was due to the terrible effects of the First World War.'*

*'It was due to the mistakes made by the Provisional Government'.*

*'It was Lenin's skill and determination that caused it.'*

*'It was because the different revolutionary groups could not work together.'*

Then read your short paragraphs to a neighbour. Get them to score each one according to how convincing they think it is as an interpretation: 1 = not very convincing, 5 = very convincing.

## Activity ?

When trying to make sense of the events of 1917 in Russia, historians rely on a number of different types of evidence as sources of information. Some of these are listed here. For each type of evidence, suggest its **strengths** and **weaknesses** for discovering exactly what occurred in 1917 and why.

| Type of evidence available as a source of information for what happened in 1917 | Strength as evidence | Weakness as evidence |
| --- | --- | --- |
| Paintings produced under later communist rule. | | |
| Speeches made at the time by political leaders. | | |
| Memoirs written later by those present in 1917. | | |
| Newspapers produced in 1917 by political parties. | | |
| Photographs taken in Petrograd in 1917. | | |
| Reports by foreign diplomats in Russia in 1917. | | |

## Writing historically: organising ideas

The most successful historical writing is clearly organised, guiding the reader through the writer's ideas.

### Learning outcomes

By the end of this lesson, you will understand how to:

- organise your ideas into paragraphs
- link your paragraphs to guide the reader.

### Definitions

**Paragraph:** a unit of text that focuses on a particular point or idea and related information.

**How can I organise my ideas into paragraphs?**

Look at the notes below written in response to this exam-style question:

> Explain the problems facing the tsar in early 1917. **(12 marks)**

Casualties – the suffering caused by the war

Political failures – tsar's refusal to share more power with duma

Economic problems – disruption of trade, rising prices

Conditions in towns over winter – food shortages, angry population

Demonstrations of early 1917 – huge numbers on the streets of Petrograd

Final crisis – tsar's decision to order the military to disperse protesters

Tsar's mistake in becoming commander-in-chief – carrying the blame

Now look at the full response below.

> The First World War put the tsarist system of government under tremendous strain and revealed how badly the country was run. After early successes, huge casualty figures made many people unwilling to continue with the war. This was made worse by the tsar's decision to become commander-in-chief, which both meant that he could be blamed for military losses and was far away from Petrograd at army headquarters. People's suffering was increased by disruptions to agriculture and trade that caused prices to increase in the towns and cities. Over the winter of 1916–17 the tsar was facing increasing problems, due to an angry population that was demanding change.
>
> In the early months of 1917, problems increased due to food shortages over a very cold winter. But the tsar managed to make his problems worse by refusing to include the duma more in the running of the country and the war. With an improvement in the weather, huge numbers of demonstrators took to the streets in February. This was a direct threat to the tsar but he made matters worse by ordering the military to disperse the protesters. This led to regiments mutinying and the tsar losing control.

**1.** a. What is the key focus of each of these paragraphs?

   b. Why do you think this response chose to focus on these two key areas?

   c. Why do you think this response chose to sequence these two paragraphs in this order?

   d. Which points in the notes have not been included in the final response? Why do you think the writer decided not to include them?

**2.** Look closely at the structure of the first paragraph. Which sentences:

   a. clearly indicate the central topic of the paragraph

   b. show knowledge and understanding of that topic

   c. explain its significance to the question?

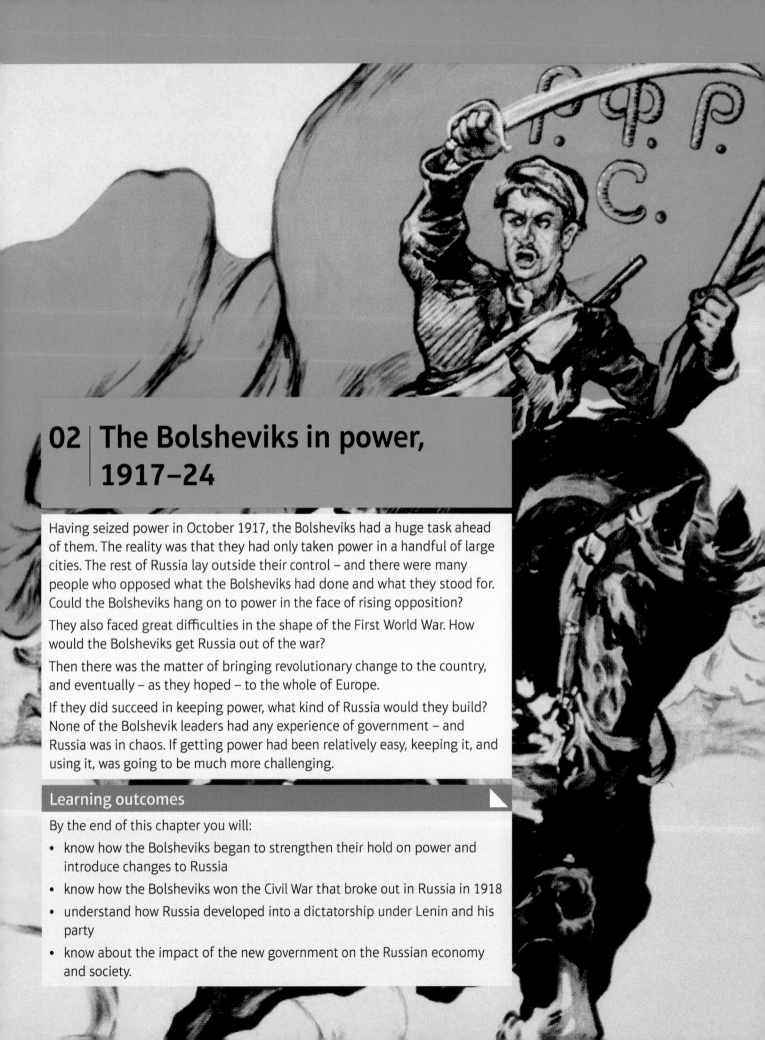

# 02 | The Bolsheviks in power, 1917–24

Having seized power in October 1917, the Bolsheviks had a huge task ahead of them. The reality was that they had only taken power in a handful of large cities. The rest of Russia lay outside their control – and there were many people who opposed what the Bolsheviks had done and what they stood for. Could the Bolsheviks hang on to power in the face of rising opposition?

They also faced great difficulties in the shape of the First World War. How would the Bolsheviks get Russia out of the war?

Then there was the matter of bringing revolutionary change to the country, and eventually – as they hoped – to the whole of Europe.

If they did succeed in keeping power, what kind of Russia would they build? None of the Bolshevik leaders had any experience of government – and Russia was in chaos. If getting power had been relatively easy, keeping it, and using it, was going to be much more challenging.

## Learning outcomes

By the end of this chapter you will:

- know how the Bolsheviks began to strengthen their hold on power and introduce changes to Russia
- know how the Bolsheviks won the Civil War that broke out in Russia in 1918
- understand how Russia developed into a dictatorship under Lenin and his party
- know about the impact of the new government on the Russian economy and society.

# 2.1 Early consolidation of power, 1917–18

- Know how the Bolsheviks secured their hold on power.
- Understand how securing power was connected with getting out of the First World War.
- Understand the impact of the Bolsheviks' actions on their opponents.

## Timeline
### From Bolshevik rule to the USSR, 1917–1924

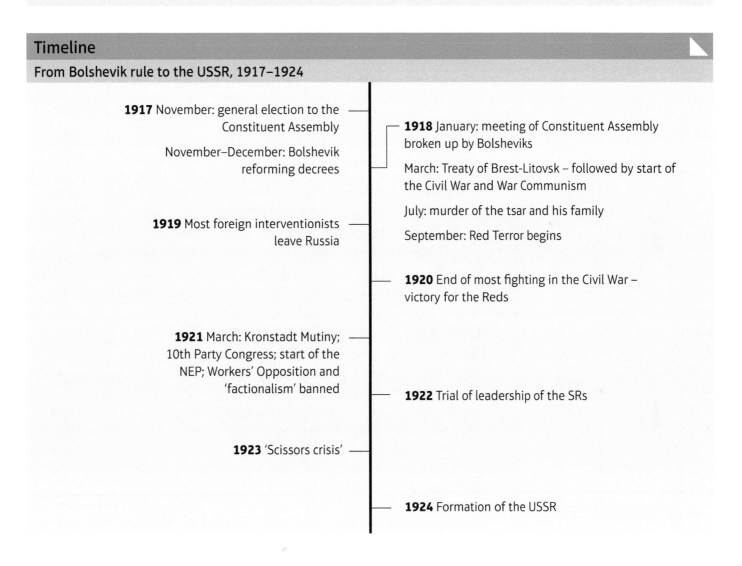

**1917** November: general election to the Constituent Assembly

November–December: Bolshevik reforming decrees

**1918** January: meeting of Constituent Assembly broken up by Bolsheviks

March: Treaty of Brest-Litovsk – followed by start of the Civil War and War Communism

July: murder of the tsar and his family

September: Red Terror begins

**1919** Most foreign interventionists leave Russia

**1920** End of most fighting in the Civil War – victory for the Reds

**1921** March: Kronstadt Mutiny; 10th Party Congress; start of the NEP; Workers' Opposition and 'factionalism' banned

**1922** Trial of leadership of the SRs

**1923** 'Scissors crisis'

**1924** Formation of the USSR

## The early Bolshevik decrees of November–December 1917

When the Bolsheviks seized power from the Provisional Government, in October 1917, they claimed they were doing so on behalf of the workers, peasants and soldiers of Russia. They condemned the previous government for failing to reform Russia or take them out of the war. Having taken power, the Bolsheviks were determined to show the people of Russia that they were capable of bringing in these great changes. They began to do so with a series of important laws – or decrees.

## The Decree on Peace, November 1917

This was the first decree passed by the All-Russian Congress of Soviets after the Bolsheviks had seized power. It called for all countries involved in the war to immediately begin peace negotiations. The aim was to create peace 'without annexations and indemnities'. This meant that no country's land was to be seized by another, and no country would punish another with massive fines. This increased support for the Bolsheviks among the Russian army and civilians. The Bolsheviks also hoped that it might encourage German soldiers to begin their own Bolshevik-style revolution, and spread it across Europe. This didn't happen.

### The Decree on Land, November 1917

That same day – 8 November – a decree distributed the land of wealthy landowners to the peasants. Many peasants had taken this land already – but the decree gave this the force of law, and indicated that the new Bolshevik government approved of the land seizures. Land redistribution was something that the Provisional Government had failed to do – and this had lost it a lot of peasant support.

In December, the Bolsheviks went further and nationalised* Church land. At the same time, many Russian churches were damaged or shut.

### Decrees on workers' rights

In November and December 1917, several more decrees were published, which aimed to improve the lives of workers in the Russian towns and cities:

- The **Decree on Work** introduced an eight-hour working day and a forty-eight hour week – to give workers less demanding hours.
- The **Decree on Unemployment** brought in unemployment insurance – to support workers who found themselves injured, ill or unemployed.
- The **Decree on Workers' Control** allowed workers' committees to run their factories – many workers had already seized control of their workplaces.

### Decree on Nationalities, November 1917

This promised all the different peoples of the old tsarist Russian empire that they could have their own governments – of their own choice. No longer would Russian rule and the Russian language be forced on the different peoples of the Russian empire – who included Ukrainians, Georgians, Armenians, Poles, and many others. This was an attempt to stop these nations breaking away and becoming independent. It seemed as though the Decree on Nationalities would give these groups more rights – but, in reality, they actually became more tightly controlled under Bolshevik rule than ever before.

### The soviets' response to the Bolshevik decrees

The Bolshevik decrees gained them increased support from across the system of soviets: it seemed that a new kind of Russia was emerging – one in which those who were unhappy with the 'old Russia' would finally find things changing in ways that benefitted them.

In November, all titles had been abolished: people would no longer be addressed by titles like 'Your honour' or 'Your Excellency'. From this point onwards, everyone would simply be described as 'Comrade'. It seemed that a classless society was emerging.

These changes encouraged those soviets which were not run by Bolsheviks to accept the new government and support its right to rule. This was important because, at first, the Bolsheviks did not control every soviet.

---

**Key term**

**Nationalise***

Take over an organisation or property to be run by the government.

---

**Peace:**
the decrees took Russia out of the First World War.

**Industry:**
working hours and conditions for workers improved.

**Impact of the November 1917 Bolshevik decrees**

**Rights for non-Russians:**
non-Russian people (e.g. Ukrainians, Georgians) were promised equal rights and the right to use their own language.

**Land:**
peasants were allowed to seize land.

**Figure 2.1** Areas of life affected by the Bolshevik decrees of 1917.

# Dealing with political opponents

## The election of the Constituent Assembly

The Provisional Government had put off calling a general election (see page 25), and it was overthrown by the Bolsheviks before an election had been arranged.

The Bolsheviks were also reluctant to organise elections, as they did not intend to set up a parliamentary democracy*. Their real intention was to work through the soviets that they controlled. However, there was a great expectation that a general election should be held – so Lenin finally agreed. In November 1917, 41.7 million people voted in the long-awaited election.

**Key term**

**Parliamentary democracy***
A system of government in which voters choose freely between a number of political parties, and the party that gains the most seats in parliament forms the government.

The results were a disappointment to the Bolsheviks – who only won 168 seats. In contrast, the Socialist Revolutionaries (SRs) gained 370 seats. Some SRs (the Left SRs) actually supported the Bolsheviks; but, nevertheless, the results were not good for the Bolsheviks – they had won less than 25% of the vote, while the various SRs gained just over 40% of all votes. The remaining votes were split between other parties – such as Mensheviks, anarchists*, Kadets and others. Those who were elected, expected to sit in a new parliamentary body called the Constituent Assembly.

## Key term

**Anarchists***

People who oppose all central government and try to create a stateless society of self-governing local communities.

## Source A

An announcement made by Sovnarkom – the central council representing the All-Russian Congress of Soviets – in November 1917. Lenin was the chair of Sovnarkom.

```
There is no place for enemies of the people,
landowners and capitalists in the Constituent
Assembly! The country can be saved only by
a Constituent Assembly of representatives
of the toiling and exploited classes of the
people! Long live the revolution! Long live
the soviets! Long live peace!
```

## Source B

An announcement made by Sovnarkom in November 1917, banning the Kadet Party.

```
Sovnarkom declares the Constitutional
Democratic Party [Kadet Party], an
organisation of counter-revolutionary
revolt, to be a party of enemies of the
people. The political leaders of the counter-
revolutionary civil war will be arrested.
```

## The Bolsheviks abolish the Constituent Assembly

The Constituent Assembly finally met in January 1918 – but the Bolsheviks had no intention of letting it continue. They had no control over the assembly – and they had no intention of giving up the power that they had seized in October 1917. So, after just one day, the assembly was broken up by Bolshevik Red Guards and sailors from the Baltic Fleet at Kronstadt.

## Source C

A declaration by the Menshevik Party on 5 January 1918, on the opening day of the Constituent Assembly.

```
The Constituent Assembly is gathering at a
time when the whole country is enveloped in
the flames of civil war and all democratic
freedoms have been suppressed, when...
freedom of speech, assembly, unions and
even the right to strike do not exist,
when the prisons are full of experienced
revolutionaries, socialists and even members
of the Constituent Assembly itself, when
there is no justice.
```

## Activities ?

1   What impression do you get from Sources A and B about Lenin's attitude towards the elections to the Constituent Assembly and towards rival political parties?

2   Would the writer of Source C have agreed or disagreed with Lenin's outlook? Why?

3   Using these three sources, and other information, explain what Lenin and the Bolsheviks had against the Constituent Assembly.

## The end of democracy in Russia?

The end of the Constituent Assembly signalled the end of democracy in Russia. With the assembly disbanded, the Bolsheviks set about consolidating their one-party control over Russia. They used the Russian railway network to spread Bolshevik control to the main cities of central Russia. In areas where there were soviets that did not accept the rule of the Bolsheviks, they were now brought under direct control by force. Historians sometimes refer to this as the 'Railway War'.

At first Lenin's government – represented by Sovnarkom (short for 'Council of People's Commissars') – included Left SRs as well as Bolsheviks. This alliance lasted until March 1917. It broke down when the Left SRs refused to accept the Bolshevik decision to sign the Treaty of Brest-Litovsk (see page 48), with Germany, in order to get Russia out of the First World War.

## Interpretation 1

From *The Soviet Union a Documentary Reader, 1917–1940*, by E. Acton and T. Stableford, published in 2005.

*Once it was clear that the Bolsheviks and their Left SR allies would be heavily outnumbered, Lenin and the leadership... began to downgrade the Assembly. He insisted that it must come to terms with the reality of Soviet power... A new date (5 January 1918) was set for the Assembly to convene, but at the same time, to underline that the Soviet order was here to stay, a third All-Russian Soviet Congress was summoned to meet three days later.*

## Interpretation 2

From *The Russian Revolution from Lenin to Stalin, 1917–1929*, by E.H. Carr, published in 1979.

*When the deputies [of the Constituent Assembly] met in January 1918 the Workers' and Peasants' Government [the Bolsheviks] was firmly established in Petrograd, and was unlikely to abdicate in favour of a body which represented the confused moods of the countryside two months earlier.*

## Exam-style question, Section B

Study Interpretations 1 and 2. They give different views about the end of the Constituent Assembly. What is the main difference between these views?

Explain your answer using details from both interpretations. **4 marks**

## Exam tip

Think about specific reasons given in the interpretations, and identify ways in which these indicate different explanations for the refusal of the Bolsheviks to accept the assembly.

## The execution of the Romanovs

After Tsar Nicholas II abdicated, he and his family were closely guarded and were moved out of Petrograd to prevent any rescue attempts. Finally, they were taken to the Ipatiev House in Yekaterinburg in the Ural Mountains.

The tsar had hoped that he and his family would be allowed to leave Russia; but neither the French nor the British (even though the tsar was related to George V) would allow them to enter their countries. Although France and Britain had once been Nicholas's close allies, they now found him an embarrassment. They claimed that, as they were fighting a war to defend democracy, they could not help someone who had ruled as an autocrat* – even though they had been allies with Russia before Nicholas abdicated.

## Key term

**Autocrat***
A ruler who holds all the power, and does not consult with or work with others.

When the Provisional Government was overthrown by the Bolsheviks, in October 1917, the tsar and his family found themselves under Bolshevik control. The local Urals soviet became responsible for guarding them. There was talk of putting the tsar on trial, but this did not happen.

By the summer of 1918, Civil War* had broken out in Russia, and the Bolsheviks were fighting for survival. They feared that one of the anti-Bolshevik armies advancing through the Urals area might free the tsar. So, on 17 July 1918, Nicholas II and his entire family, their remaining servants and their doctor, were taken down into the cellar and murdered by Bolsheviks on the orders of Lenin's government in Moscow. This ended more than three centuries of the Romanov family's rule in Russia, and made it certain that Russia would have to find a new system of government.

## Key term

**Civil war***
A war in which both sides are from the same country.

# Taking Russia out of the First World War: the Treaty of Brest-Litovsk

The Bolsheviks had promised to end Russia's involvement in the First World War; and the job of negotiating the end of the fighting was given to Trotsky as Commissar for War. Trotsky had hoped Russia could avoid continuing to fight the war; but he also wished to avoid surrendering, because the Germans were making huge demands on Russia. He hoped for a middle way: 'no peace, no war'.

Trotsky was to be disappointed. The Germans kept advancing, and Petrograd seemed in danger of being captured. The capital was moved to Moscow (and has stayed there ever since). The so-called 'Left Communists' wanted to continue the war, but Lenin finally persuaded his colleagues to agree to the German terms. The Left SRs walked out in protest. Now the government was entirely Bolshevik.

In March 1918, the Treaty of Brest-Litovsk was signed with Germany. The main outcomes of the treaty were:

- Russia lost all its western lands: Finland, Estonia, Latvia, Lithuania, Ukraine and parts of Poland; it also lost Georgia
- Russia lost 62 million people – or 26% of its population
- Russia lost 27% of its farmland, 26% of its railways, and 74% of its iron ore and coal
- Russia had to pay Germany 300 million gold roubles.

## Source D

A photograph taken in 1918, showing Trotsky with German representatives arriving at the Brest-Litovsk treaty negotiations.

## Reasons for the Treaty of Brest-Litovsk

The Bolsheviks had agreed to the treaty for a number of reasons:

- They needed a 'breathing space' – a chance to get their rule organised without being overwhelmed by the military and economic problems caused by continuing to fight the war. It was continuing with the war that had undermined the tsar and the Provisional Government.

- They also realised that there were many groups in Russia opposed to them. If Bolshevik rule was to survive, it needed to concentrate all its attention on strengthening its hold on Russia, increasing its support, and preparing to defend itself against the threats it faced **within** Russia.

- The Bolsheviks hoped that revolution would soon break out across Europe – and the treaty they signed would then be torn up.

### Activity ?

Imagine you are Lenin in March 1918. You know that the Treaty of Brest-Litovsk is going to be very unpopular. Write a speech in which you explain why you think that it is necessary to sign it. You can refer to the terrible cost of it – but you must try to persuade people it should still happen.

## THINKING HISTORICALLY  Cause and consequence (6a)

### Seeing things differently

Different times and different places have different sets of ideas. Beliefs about how the world works, how human societies should be governed, or the best way to achieve economic prosperity, can all be radically different from our own. It is important for the historian to take into account these different attitudes when examining people's reactions and motivations in the past.

### The killing of the tsar and his family

In 1918, the Bolsheviks killed the tsar and his family. Many people today, in Russia and elsewhere, view this act with horror. At the time, the Bolsheviks believed that this was justified because they feared the tsar might become a figurehead for the Whites (anti-Bolshevik forces). Local Bolsheviks were aware there were White armies nearby. The leaders in Moscow also believed that, as revolutionaries, they had the right to sweep away all that survived from the old Russia. There was no trial, and the Bolsheviks had no respect for ideas such as 'the rule of law'. Equally shocking is the fact that the governments of Britain and France had refused to take the tsar and his family in.

1  Imagine that a modern foreign government decided to kill a ruler who had been overthrown, along with his entire family.

   a  What would be the reaction of the government here in Britain?

   b  What would be the reaction of supporters of the executed ruler?

   c  What would be the reaction of the press and the general public here in Britain?

2  Bolshevik attitudes to law and execution were different to current attitudes in Britain.

   a  Write one sentence explaining the importance to the Bolsheviks of removing all that survived from the old Russia. Then write one sentence explaining how people in Britain nowadays might think that a ruler who had been overthrown should be treated.

   b  Write one sentence explaining the importance of 'the rule of law' to the Bolsheviks. Then write one sentence explaining the importance of 'the rule of law' to most ordinary people in a modern democracy.

3  Write a paragraph explaining how Bolshevik attitudes towards revolution and 'the rule of law' contributed to the killing of the tsar and his family. Remember to refer to both the attitudes of the government and the attitudes of ordinary Bolsheviks carrying out the killing.

**Figure 2.2** The impact of the Treaty of Brest-Litovsk on Russia.

## Reactions to the treaty in Russia

In a sense, the treaty saved the Bolshevik government – as they could not have continued to fight the war – and soldiers were relieved that the fighting seemed to be over. But it was also a crushing blow to Russia, and encouraged the Bolsheviks' enemies to try and overthrow their government and restore Russian greatness. The Left SRs even assassinated* the German ambassador to Russia in the hope of starting the war again.

### Key term

**Assassinate***

Murder somebody for political reasons.

Most horrified of all were the nationalists. Russia had been humiliated and had lost huge amounts of its territory. The Russian empire in the west had been stripped of its most valuable regions. The nationalists began to form themselves into 'White Armies' to overthrow the 'Reds' (the Bolsheviks) and – in their view – save Russia. For Russia, the end of the First World War began a slide towards Civil War.

## Summary

- The Bolsheviks began to change Russia through a series of revolutionary decrees.
- They failed to get sufficient votes in a general election and so shut down the Constituent Assembly.
- They pulled Russia out of the First World War – even though this came at a high price.
- The tsar and his entire family were murdered, so that opposition to the Bolsheviks could not form around them.

## Checkpoint

### Strengthen

**S1** Create a spidergram of the decrees passed by the Bolsheviks in late 1917. By each decree, make a note of how it was intended to change Russia.

**S2** The Treaty of Brest-Litovsk cost Russia a great deal. Explain to a neighbour why the Bolsheviks thought it was a price worth paying.

### Challenge

**C1** Which of the decrees passed by the Bolsheviks, in their first two months in power, do you think was the most important in changing Russia? Explain your choice.

**C2** Russia was desperate to get out of the First World War – so why did the Treaty of Brest-Litovsk cause the Bolsheviks so much trouble?

**C3** Explain why the Bolsheviks refused to accept the authority of the Constituent Assembly, and what this reveals about the kind of government that would emerge under their rule.

How confident do you feel about your answers to these questions? If you are unsure, read your answers to a neighbour and get them to suggest improvements.

# 2.2 The Civil War, 1918–21

## Learning outcomes

- Know the different groups that fought in the Russian Civil War.
- Know the main events of the Civil War.
- Understand why the 'Reds' won the Civil War.

By 1918, the old tsarist empire was falling apart. In the west, Finland, Estonia, Latvia and Lithuania had declared themselves free from Russian rule. Across what remained of the Russian empire, different groups began to arm themselves to resist the Bolsheviks. This led to the Civil War.

## Who fought in the Civil War?

There were several different groups fighting each other for control over Russia in the Civil War. They are often described using colours.

There were also armies fighting to free their nations from Russian control – for example in Finland and Georgia.

**Figure 2.3** The main groups fighting in the Russian Civil War.

51

## Extend your knowledge

**A Ukrainian anarchist: Nestor Makhno**

In southern Ukraine an anarchist leader named Nestor Makhno, and his Revolutionary Insurrectionary Army of Ukraine, fought, in turn: the Reds, the Whites, Germans, Austrians, Ukrainian nationalists and Cossacks (semi-independent communities who offered military service to the tsar and later opposed the Reds). This illustrates how complex and confusing the Russian Civil War was. In the end, Makhno was defeated by the Reds, left Russia, and died in Paris in 1934.

# Why was there Civil War in Russia?

Nationalists and conservatives were determined to overthrow the Bolsheviks. They opposed their plans for social change, workers' influence in industry, and peasant seizure of land from landlords. Most of all they opposed the Bolsheviks for signing the Treaty of Brest-Litovsk. Some monarchists* wished to restore the tsar. Middle-class Russians feared the loss of their wealth and influence.

Left wing groups – like the Mensheviks and more moderate SRs – resented the Bolsheviks for abolishing the Constituent Assembly and setting up a dictatorship. Even members of some soviets were becoming disillusioned with how the Bolsheviks were imposing control on them.

## Key term

**Monarchists***
Those who believe a country should be run by a king or queen.

An unlikely force, that became increasingly important in the drift towards Civil War, was the 'Czech Legion'. These were about 40,000 Czech soldiers, from the Austro-Hungarian army, who had been captured in the First World War as they fought the Russians. Czechs were one of the many nationalities that made up the

## Source A

A Soviet recruitment poster from the 1920s, calling on working class men to join the Red Army cavalry.

Austro-Hungarian Empire. They hoped that their country might at last become independent, and so switched sides to fight for the Russians against the Austrians and Germans. After the Treaty of Brest-Litovsk, they hoped to travel across Russia on the Trans-Siberian Railway, then use ships from Vladivostok to sail round the world and fight on the Western Front – beside the British and French – against the Germans.

However, the Bolsheviks didn't trust the Czechs, and tried to take away their weapons. When the Czechs fought back, they found themselves controlling the Trans-Siberian Railway. Many anti-Bolshevik forces joined them, and were encouraged to fight the Reds by the British and French – who hoped to get Russia back into the First World War.

# Key events of the Civil War

There were three main White armies facing the Bolsheviks:

- In the Ural Mountains and Siberia, there was a White army commanded by Admiral Kolchak. He set up a Siberian Regional Government in the city of Omsk. His army had some successes against the Reds, until a counter-attack broke its power in the summer of 1919.

- In southern Russia, there was a White army led by General Denikin – known as the Armed Forces of Southern Russia. To begin with, Denikin's army was successful, and advanced to within 240 kilometres of Moscow; but the Reds fought it off and it was forced to retreat in 1920. Denikin resigned, and was replaced by Baron Wrangel. By the end of 1920, what remained of this army was evacuated from the Crimea by British and French ships.

- In the north-west, based in Estonia, was a White army led by General Yudenich. In October 1919, this army almost captured Petrograd, but was defeated by the Red Army, led by Trotsky.

As well as fighting the Whites in the Civil War, the Reds had to fight a number of wars against the Greens, and nationalities trying to break away from Russian control. Estonia, Latvia and Lithuania all succeeded – but Ukraine, Armenia, Georgia and Azerbaijan were eventually defeated and forced to return to Russian control. This fighting lasted from 1918 until 1921 – even after the Whites had been defeated.

## Source B

Bank note produced in southern Russia by the White government of General Denikin, in 1919. The figure of St George killing a dragon or serpent was a traditional Russian symbol, and the double-headed eagle and flag were symbols of tsarist Russia.

## Source C

From a manifesto issued by the White leader, Admiral Kolchak, in November 1918.

Taking up the cross [taking on a burden, or making a sacrifice, like Jesus Christ] of this power in the exceptionally difficult conditions of civil war... I declare that I will not go either on the road of reaction [opposing all change] or on the fatal road of party politics. I set as my chief aim... the establishment of law and order, so that the people can choose for itself, without obstruction, the form of government which it desires and realise the great ideals of liberty.

**Key**
- Held by Bolsheviks, February 1918
- Held by Bolsheviks, summer 1918
- New countries, breaking free from Russia
- **Makhno** Greens
- **Kolchak** Whites

Finland
Estonia
**Yudenich**
Latvia
Lithuania
Poland
**Kolchak**
Baltic Sea
**Makhno**
**Wrangel**
**Denikin**
Black Sea
Georgia
Azerbaijan
Armenia
Caspian Sea
N
0    200
km

**Figure 2.4** The main areas of conflict in the Russian Civil War.

## THINKING HISTORICALLY   Evidence (3b)

**It depends on the question**

When considering the usefulness of historical sources, people often consider 'reliability' (whether a witness can be trusted). This is important – but some sources are not witnesses, they are simply the remains of the past.

Work in small groups.

1 Imagine you are investigating how the Whites tried to present themselves as representatives of traditional Russian values and traditions. Look at Source B:

   **a** Write at least two statements that you can reasonably infer about the character of the Whites based solely on Source B.

   **b** Which of your statements are you most sure of? Explain your answer.

2 Source C is unreliable testimony – its author was trying to persuade others. Try to think of at least two statements that you can still reasonably infer about the character of the Whites using this source.

3 Which source is more useful for investigating how the Whites presented their character and beliefs? Explain your answer.

4 In your group, discuss the following question and write down your thoughts: How are reliability and usefulness related?

## Bolshevik (Red) strengths

The Bolsheviks had several advantages over the Whites and Greens that helped them to come out of the Civil War on top:

- They controlled central Russia (see Figure 2.4). This meant they had much shorter distances over which to supply their armies. Their area also contained most of the population – who could be made to join the Red Army or work for the Bolsheviks.

- The Bolsheviks formed their own powerful fighting force: the Red Army. They used conscription* to fill its ranks – and by 1920 it was over five million strong!

- In time, the Red Army became noted for its discipline and unity. Trotsky was in command of the army and proved to be an effective leader.

- The Bolsheviks controlled most of Russia's industry and the railways that radiated out from Moscow. This helped them to produce and move weapons.

- The Bolsheviks worked hard to win supporters. Using propaganda* they presented themselves as the only force that would change the lives of ordinary Russians for the better. They claimed that the Whites would turn the clock back and stop any reforms. A government organisation – called Agitprop – spread the message with plays, films and posters carried around the country on trains and river steamers.

- Making and breaking alliances – with anarchists and other Greens – meant that they did not have to fight all their enemies at the same time.

## Key terms

**Conscription***
Being made to join the armed forces.

**Propaganda***
Information deliberately used to influence an audience and persuade them that a particular view is correct.

**Mobilisation***
Creating and organising an army.

**Front***
An area where two sides in a conflict are fighting.

### Trotsky as commander of the Red Army

As commander of the Red Army, Trotsky was more important than Lenin in winning the Civil War. It was Trotsky, in 1918, who organised the mass mobilisation* of workers and peasants to form the Red Army. He had immense energy and enthusiasm and travelled huge distances – from front* to front – in a special train.

## Extend your knowledge

### Trotsky's war train

On Trotsky's train there were about 250 people. These included: bodyguards; a machine gun unit; radio and telegraph operators; workmen to repair the tracks; and printing press operators, so that he could produce leaflets and newspapers to spread ideas and encourage support. The train was a mobile war-fighting and propaganda-producing machine.

Recognising that the Bolsheviks lacked military experience, Trotsky was prepared to employ ex-tsarist officers. This was unpopular with many Bolsheviks, but Lenin and Trotsky knew that it was necessary. Trotsky made sure of their loyalty by introducing commissars* and by holding the officers' families hostage*.

## Key terms

### Commissar*

Political officer in the Red Army, with the job of encouraging Bolshevik ideas among ordinary soldiers and keeping an eye on ex-tsarist officers.

### Hostage*

A person held as a prisoner to make somebody else do as the hostage-takers want. In the Civil War, ex-tsarist officers' families were taken hostage. If the officer deserted the Red Army, then his family would be punished.

### Deserters*

Soldiers who run away from battle or from their units.

### Literacy*

The ability to read and write.

### Oath*

A solemn promise.

Trotsky also introduced strict discipline into the Red Army – in contrast to the chaos of 1917. Deserters* were shot, and units that retreated had one in ten men shot (decimated). Alongside the discipline, Trotsky encouraged education in the Red Army. This involved both education in literacy*, and political education about the ideas and aims of the Bolsheviks.

To encourage loyalty he had all Red Army soldiers swear the Socialist Military Oath* which said how they would behave as soldiers of the Red Army. He also brought in a special medal – the Red Banner – to reward ordinary soldiers who fought bravely.

As in October 1917, it was Trotsky who organised much of the action but it was Lenin who provided the vital driving leadership and direction.

## Source D

A Bolshevik poster from 1918. The figure in the centre represents Trotsky and the dragon represents capitalism. The text on its body says 'counter-revolution'.

## Activities

1 Look at Sources B and D. What is the poster Source D saying about Trotsky? Link your answers to details on the poster and refer to the use of St. George on Source B.

2 Why did the Bolsheviks choose to depict Trotsky in this way? Does this surprise you?

3 Explain how the following helped the Reds to present Trotsky and the Red Army in this way:

   a Foreign intervention.

   b The behaviour of the Whites.

   c Promises made by the Bolsheviks.

## Weaknesses of the Whites

The Whites had several disadvantages compared to the Reds, which made it impossible for them to win the Civil War:

- They were geographically too spread out. They had to travel much larger distances to supply their armies than the Reds did.
- They controlled few areas with industry or natural resources that could supply their armies.
- There were far fewer Whites than Reds: at the most their armies had 250,000 fighting men.
- Many White armies were linked to a particular area and would not fight beyond it.
- There was no single White leader who the opposition to the Bolsheviks could unite around. The different White leaders were in competition with each other.
- The Whites had no common plan for Russia. There were divisions between monarchists, liberals and left wing groups.
- The Whites were unpopular because they treated peasants badly and planned to force non-Russians back under Russian control. Many Whites wanted to turn back the clock, which frightened workers and peasants: if the Whites won, they would lose many advantages they had gained under the Bolsheviks.

### *Foreign intervention*

The Whites were helped by foreign intervention. British, French, US and Japanese soldiers were landed at various places on the outer fringes of Russia. Their goals were to encourage the Whites to fight the Reds, and to prevent stores of weapons and ammunition donated to the Whites by the Allies from falling into Bolshevik hands. These foreign countries wanted to prevent the spread of Bolshevik ideas to other countries. Most foreign forces had been withdrawn from Russia by the middle of 1919, but their intervention gave the Whites a boost for a time – which made them seem stronger than they really were.

Foreign support for the Whites played into the Bolsheviks hands. It meant the Bolsheviks could appeal to Russian national pride. Many patriotic Russians – who might otherwise have supported the Whites – were prepared to support the Reds after the Whites accepted foreign help.

### Source E

A poster issued by the Bolsheviks in 1920. The text says, 'You – have you volunteered yet?'

### Source F

The view of the SR leader Lebedev on the need to capture Moscow from a collection of his writings on the Civil War, published in 1928.

All her resources of people, of war, of finance would now be in our hands. In Moscow we would get masses of troops, there we would get the whole brain of our country, all her soul, all that is talented in Russia.

### Source G

From comments made by the British politician Winston Churchill in a book about the Russian Civil War, published in 1929.

The ancient capital [Moscow] lay at the centre of a web of railroads... and in the midst a spider! Vain hope to crush the spider by the advance of lines of encircling flies.

## Activities ?

1  According to Source F, what great advantage did the Bolsheviks have? Why was this an advantage?

2  To what extent does the evidence in Sources E and G agree with the view expressed in Source F? Explain your answer by referring to all three sources.

3  Using Sources D, E and F, and other information in this section, explain why the Reds won the Russian Civil War. Group different reasons into short paragraphs and, finally, conclude with the most important reason, and why you think this was so important.

# Effects of the Civil War

Victory in the Civil War made the Bolsheviks certain that their view of the world was right. Although revolution had not spread across Europe, their confidence was boosted by their success.

The Civil War had also made the Bolsheviks more reliant on using force and terror to gain control. By the end of 1918, there were units of the Cheka (Bolshevik political police) in every area that the Reds controlled. The Cheka arrested and shot anyone it considered an enemy (see page 59).

Fighting the Civil War also made the Bolsheviks more organised, with tight central control under a strong leadership. Lenin had already begun this process, but the war strengthened it. It also accelerated the destruction of rival political groups.

However, the Civil War exhausted Russia: millions of people had died; the economy was badly damaged; and the populations of major cities had dropped by half, as people left to escape food shortages.

In addition, the brutal behaviour of the Bolsheviks had led to protests within the party (see 'The Workers' Opposition', page 66) and from people who had previously supported the revolution (see the Kronstadt Mutiny, page 60). Across Russia, peasants protested at the way Bolsheviks seized their grain and shot opponents.

The Reds had won the Civil War – but it was not at all clear what kind of Russia would develop in the 1920s.

## Summary

- Civil War broke out in Russia in opposition to the way the Bolsheviks were running the country.
- Opposition forces were divided – both politically and geographically.
- The Reds had a number of advantages – and were skilful at making the most of them.
- The Whites faced a number of disadvantages – and never overcame them.

## Checkpoint

### Strengthen

**S1** List at least three reasons why a Civil War broke out in Russia.

**S2** Construct a spidergram summarising the strengths of the Reds. Colour code it for: Political, Military, Social and Economic factors.

**S3** Make a similar spidergram summarising the weaknesses of the Whites.

### Challenge

**C1** Write a definition of each of the following groups who fought in the Russian Civil War: Reds, Whites, Greens. Include information on their ideas and beliefs.

**C2** From the information in this section, explain why some historians think that the Reds were always going to win the Civil War – even though they faced many enemies.

**C3** Choose the single most important reason why the Reds won. Explain your choice.

If you are not confident about your answers to these questions, discuss them with your teacher and make a note of any areas in which you could improve your answers.

## Learning outcomes

- Know how the Bolsheviks treated their opponents.
- Understand the role of the Cheka and 'terror'.
- Understand how this increased the power of the Bolshevik dictatorship.

## Key terms

**Show trial***

A trial that is deliberately given a lot of publicity, to spread a message to the population.

**Deported***

Forced to leave a country.

**Totalitarian***

Absolute: in a totalitarian state one organisation has complete control. In Russia – after the 1917 revolution – this one organisation was the Bolsheviks.

## Bolshevism and dictatorship

Soon after taking power, the Bolsheviks began to restrict freedom, in order to secure their control over Russia and shut down any opposition. In December 1917, they banned all non-Bolshevik newspapers. Also in December, they banned the Kadet Party and arrested its leaders – putting Russia on the path to becoming a one-party state. The law courts and lawyers were abolished and replaced by Revolutionary Tribunals. These were brutal – and judged people more according to their class than the evidence.

From June 1918, SRs and Mensheviks were arrested; anarchists were arrested after 1919; and in 1921 all other political parties were officially banned. In 1922, there was a show trial* of leading SRs. Lenin wanted them shot – but was worried this would look bad abroad – so they were deported* instead. Russia was becoming a totalitarian* state.

## Source A

A photograph showing the trial of the leaders of the Socialist Revolutionaries (SRs) in August 1922.

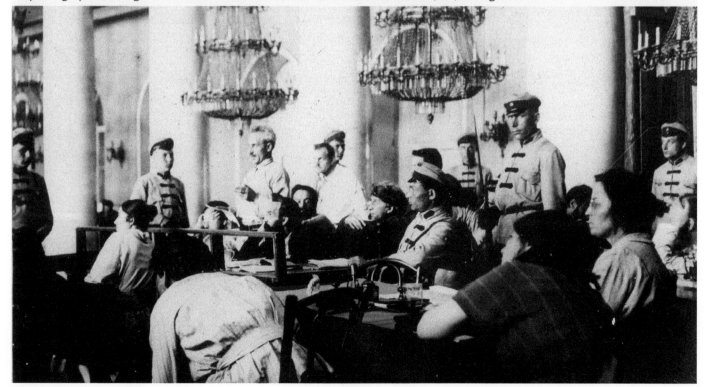

## The role of the Cheka

The Cheka's full title was: the 'Extraordinary Commission to Combat Counter-Revolution, Sabotage and Speculation'. It was set up in December 1917. It was used to arrest opposition and prevent demonstrations against the government. Its methods included executing people regarded as enemies of the revolution – usually with a single bullet to the back of the head. It was also responsible for running the political prisons that would, by the 1930s, grow into a huge system of prisons and labour camps – known as the Gulag.

In areas controlled by the Red Army, during the Civil War, terror was used to crush all opposition and remove people simply because of their social status: middle-class people, priests, nobles, and better-off peasants were all Cheka targets.

In 1922, at the end of the Civil War, the Cheka was renamed the GPU (State Political Directorate); and in 1923 the GPU became the OGPU (All-Union State Political Directorate).

### Extend your knowledge

**Commander of the Cheka – Felix Dzerzhinsky**

The first commander of the Cheka was Felix Dzerzhinsky. He came from a noble Polish family and was born when much of what is now Poland was ruled by the Russian tsar. At one time he considered becoming a Catholic priest, but instead he became a communist, while still at secondary school. Under the tsar, he was imprisoned and severely beaten by prison guards many times. Dzerzhinsky believed state-organised terror should be used to crush opposition and prevent it from occurring. He died of a heart attack in 1926, after giving a two-hour-long political speech.

## 'The Socialist Fatherland is in Danger' decree

In February 1918, the Bolsheviks passed a decree that allowed them to force anyone they chose (usually middle-class people) to do forced labour – and allowed them to execute anyone who resisted. This soon spread to include the arrest and execution of anyone regarded as an enemy of the revolution.

### Source B

An anti-Trotsky poster distributed in Russia in 1917, showing Bolsheviks murdering opponents. The red figure represents Trotsky and the caption reads: 'Peace and Liberty in Sovdepia' (Sovdepia was a nickname for the area governed by soviets).

## The 'Red Terror'

The 'Red Terror' was a time of arrests and executions between September 1918 and February 1919. Concentration camps were set up in northern Russia, on the Solevetsky Islands and, in this period, between 50,000 and 140,000 people were executed.

Lenin started the 'Red Terror' because opposition was growing to the new government and the Civil War was starting. He was also reacting to an attempted assassination attempt – in August 1918 – when an SR – named Fanya Kaplan – had tried to kill him. Lenin was wounded, but survived. Kaplan was executed without trial.

Although the 'Red Terror' officially ended in 1919, the arrests and executions continued and accompanied the setting up of a dictatorship.

A Bolshevik poster issued in 1920. The caption reads: 'Ukrainians and Russians agree: nobody is above the working man'.

## Activities

1 Describe the viewpoints of Sources B and C on Bolshevik terror. How do they differ?

2 Using Source C, and other information, describe how the Bolsheviks would have justified the use of terror.

3 'The Bolsheviks lacked popular support and so were forced to use terror in order to stay in power.' To what extent does the evidence support this view of Bolshevik rule?

# The Kronstadt Mutiny

In March 1921, sailors from the naval base at Kronstadt mutinied against the brutal rule of the Bolsheviks – which they saw as a dictatorship. In part, the mutiny was a response to 'War Communism' (see pages 64–68). Sailors from Kronstadt had helped create the revolution in 1917 – so this mutiny was a terrible shock to Lenin. By 1921, things had changed at Kronstadt – since many of the sailors of 1917 had left there to fight in the Civil War – but sailors at Kronstadt still considered themselves revolutionaries, and their unhappiness revealed how much support Lenin and his party had lost.

The sailors demanded:

• new elections to the soviets by secret ballot
• freedom of speech and freedom of the press for all left-wing socialist parties
• free trade-unions and peasant organisations
• an end to commissars (see page 55) in the army and navy
• an end to grain requisition squads seizing grain from peasants
• government restrictions on trade to be lifted.

Lenin and his supporters reacted by calling the Kronstadt sailors 'Whites' and 'counter-revolutionaries'*. This wasn't true – the sailors just felt that Russian workers and peasants were being betrayed. Many of the sailors had families who lived in the villages, and many came from the Ukraine where suffering was particularly bad. In addition, striking workers from Petrograd had appealed to the sailors for help in improving their working conditions.

Evidence that the sailors wanted to discuss changes – rather than overthrow the revolution – can be found in the fact that they revolted while their battleships were still trapped in the winter ice. Had they really wanted to overthrow the revolution, they could have waited until they could use their powerful ships against Petrograd.

## Key term

**Counter-revolutionary***
Somebody thought to be acting against, or spreading ideas, that opposed the revolution.

The mutiny was crushed. The Red Army – under the command of Trotsky, and accompanied by the Cheka – crossed the sea ice and attacked the sailors. The sailors fought back, but were defeated. Hundreds were killed, while others escaped to Finland. Many more were captured – and hundreds of these were later executed by the Cheka. Others ended up in the concentration camps of northern Russia.

The mutiny was over – but it had a very real impact on the Bolshevik government in a number of ways. It was one of the reasons why Lenin changed direction, in 1921 (see page 66), in his treatment of the peasants and in the way in which he was running the country.

## Source D

From a declaration by the sailors of the Kronstadt naval base, March 1921.

Since the present soviets do not express the will of the workers and peasants, there should be immediate re-elections to the soviets by secret ballot and unrestricted pre-election campaigning.

## Source E

Accusations made against the Kronstadt sailors by Trotsky and Lenin in March 1921.

Tools of former tsarist generals... Agents of the interventionists [foreign countries]... Both the Mensheviks and the Socialist Revolutionaries declared the Kronstadt movement to be their own...

## Activities ?

1 Make a list of factors that caused the Kronstadt Mutiny. Use Source D and other information from this section.

2 Look at the accusations made against the mutineers by Trotsky and Lenin in Source E. Does the evidence make you accept or reject their views on the sailors? Explain why.

3 In what ways does the Kronstadt Mutiny reveal differences between the Bolsheviks and some of their supporters over what they hoped the revolution would achieve? Use Sources D and E, and other information in this section, to help form your answer.

# Centralising Bolshevik power

## From 'Bolsheviks' to 'communists'

In March 1918, the Bolsheviks officially changed the name of their party to 'Russian Communist Party (of Bolsheviks)'. Although the term 'Bolsheviks' continued to be used for some time, from this point onwards this book will call them 'communists'.

They believed that their policies were building a socialist state; and that Russia would soon be the first fully communist country in the world – where everyone willingly co-operated to build a society without class, competition or repression. Instead – Russia became a brutal dictatorship.

## The role of Lenin

Lenin played a major role in organising the government. As the leading member of the Communist Party, and chairman of the Council of People's Commissars (Sovnarkom), he united the party and the government. Under him, a centralised dictatorship grew to control Russia, and keep any political rivals under control and out of power. The growth of a centralised dictatorship under the Communist Party was very much in line with how Lenin had always used power.

## The movement of power from the soviets to the Communist Party

When the Bolsheviks took power, in October 1917, they claimed they were doing so on behalf of the soviets – and especially the All-Russian Congress of Soviets, which was meeting in Petrograd as they seized power. Because the Mensheviks, and many SRs, had walked out in protest at what the Bolsheviks had done, the All-Russian Congress of Soviets was left under the control of the Bolsheviks and their allies, the Left SRs.

In reality, power was held by the Communist Party (Bolsheviks) and not by the soviets. The soviets soon became what is known as a 'rubber stamp' – who automatically agreed the decisions made by the Communist Party.

**The Communist Party**

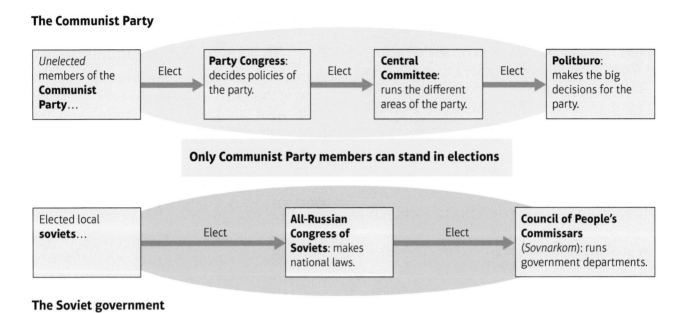

**The Soviet government**

**Figure 2.5** How the soviet government and the Communist Party worked in parallel to rule the Soviet Union.

The Soviet government looked like a democracy – but it was not – because the unelected Communist Party decided everything. It was a one-party state, without real political freedom, and people could not choose between different political ideas. The only party at elections was the Communist Party. Even if there were different individuals standing for election they could not be members of any other party. People were not allowed to criticise the Communist Party and its hold on power. Political and personal freedom was reduced as the communist dictatorship tightened its grip.

At each Party Congress, members of the whole party elected the Central Committee to make decisions until the next Party Congress. The Central Committee elected the Politburo, made up of a small number of influential people. The first Politburo's members, in 1917, were Lenin, Zinoviev, Kamenev, Trotsky and Stalin. The Politburo became increasingly powerful until the Central Committee basically went along with decisions made in the Politburo.

## Setting up the USSR: the 1924 Constitution

In 1924, the communists reorganised the lands of the old Russian empire – which they now ruled – and gave them a new name. From now on they would be known as the Union of Soviet Socialist Republics – often shortened to USSR or Soviet Union. To start with, the USSR was made up of four Soviet Socialist Republics (or SSRs). The largest was called the Russian Soviet Federated Socialist Republic (RSFSR) – which was huge, and included much of the old tsarist empire, stretching from the area west of Moscow to the Pacific Ocean. West of this was the Byelorussian SSR; to the south was the Ukrainian SSR; and the fourth SSR was the Transcaucasian Republic. Over time, other SSRs were added, but the overall name, the USSR, remained the same – and Russia (the RSFSR) remained the largest and most powerful member.

The relationship between Russia and the other Soviet Socialist Republics, was officially one of communities that had voluntarily come together to form the USSR. In fact, the Red Army had carried communist power into these areas and forced them to join – none was free to leave. The parliament of the USSR was the All-Union Congress of Soviets, but it only met for a few days a year – and it, and its decisions, were controlled by the Communist Party.

In December 1925, the Communist Party changed its name to the 'All-Union Communist Party (of Bolsheviks)'. This reflected the fact that it now claimed to be the ruling party across all the various parts of the USSR (the 'Union' referred to in the party's new title).

## Interpretation 1

From *The Russian Revolution from Lenin to Stalin, 1917–1929*, by E.H. Carr, published in 1979.

*During the civil war many Mensheviks, and some SRs, joined the Bolshevik Party; many more entered the service of the regime and worked in Soviet institutions. The mass following of both parties, persistently harassed by the authorities, began to disintegrate. When the civil war ended, there was no further basis for coalition or compromise. Two thousand Mensheviks... were said to have been arrested.*

## Interpretation 2

From *The Russian Civil War*, by E. Mawdsley, published in 1987.

*The administrative methods learned in the Civil War were revived in the late 1920s with the forced collectivisation of the peasants... Stalin's famous slogan of the 1930s was a throwback to the Civil War era: 'There is no fortress Bolsheviks cannot storm.'*

## Summary

- Russia – under Lenin – soon turned into a dictatorship.
- The Cheka was used to destroy any opposition.
- Opposition to dictatorship was revealed in the Kronstadt Mutiny of 1921.
- Despite the official power of the soviets – power really lay with the Communist Party.

## Checkpoint

### Strengthen

**S1** What was the Cheka? What did it do to keep the communists in power?

**S2** Why did the Red Terror happen?

**S3** Give three key reasons why the Kronstadt sailors mutinied.

### Challenge

**C1** Why would it be a mistake to think that the new Constitution of the USSR, in 1924, gives us a clear idea of how Russia was governed by the communists?

**C2** Explain the role of the following in the way that Russia was governed: Sovnarkom, the Politburo, the Central Committee, the All-Russian Congress of Soviets.

**C3** 'The way that Lenin approached politics meant that Russia, under his rule, was always going to become a dictatorship'. To what extent do you agree with this interpretation?

How confident do you feel about your answers to these questions? If you are unsure, carry out an internet search on each of the key terms and see what additional information you can discover about them.

# **2.4** Economic and social change, 1918–24

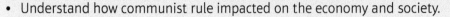
## Nationalisation and 'State Capitalism', 1917–18

When Lenin took power, his ultimate aim was to create a 'planned economy' – in which the government controlled, directed and organised all the industries of Russia. To begin with, though, it was very hard for such an inexperienced government – which, at this stage, controlled only parts of the country – to achieve this, and compromises had to be made.

One of the biggest compromises involved workers' taking control of factories. Many factories had already been taken over by workers: some were Communist Party members, loyal to Lenin – but others were not. There was little that the government could do about this at first. The 'Decree on Workers' Control', in December 1917, had allowed the takeovers, though Lenin tried to slow the process down with further decrees, in January and April 1918. However, many factory owners simply shut their factories down – rather than let them be taken over. By August 1918, about 30% of all factories were shut, and the economy was grinding to a halt.

To try to keep the economy going, the communists nationalised the biggest industries – along with banks and railways – and gave them targets for what they should be achieving. Middle-class managers and technicians were allowed to stay on in their old jobs to make sure the newly nationalised businesses were run efficiently. This approach towards the economy was called 'State Capitalism'.

Despite this, the economy continued to fall apart, and so, from the middle of 1918, a new and tougher approach was adopted – which would later be described as 'War Communism'.

## War Communism, 1918–21

There were many reasons for the government to introduce War Communism:

- Russia was drifting into Civil War; and if the communists did not get control of industry and the food supply, they would lose. Workers had to carry on producing goods – and the Red Army needed food.
- There was a strong desire in the new government to end capitalism. This involved abolishing money, the free market* and getting rid of social classes – though the distinction between workers and peasants would remain.
- Russia lost important grain-producing areas in Ukraine because of the Treaty of Brest-Litovsk. Other agricultural areas were controlled by White armies. Less and less food was reaching the cities.
- The population in the cities collapsed. Thousands went to live with their relatives in the countryside, where it was easier to get hold of food.

### Key term

**Free market***
Being able to buy and sell goods and make money with little interference or restrictions from the government.

In many ways, War Communism was what the communists were all about. When it had failed and was over, Lenin tried to suggest that it had been a temporary measure forced on the communists 'by war and ruin'. But there is plenty of evidence that it was more than this: in reality it had been an attempt to impose communist ideas.

| Measures introduced as part of War Communism | Consequences |
| --- | --- |
| A fixed price was paid for grain to keep costs down. | Peasants didn't want to sell at the lower price, so they hung onto their grain and waited for the price to improve.<br><br>The Cheka, and groups of workers, were sent to the countryside to requisition* grain from the peasants. Peasants thought to be hoarding grain were shot. |
| Food rationing was introduced. How much people received depended on what job they did. People in jobs that were central to winning the war had the best rations. | Workers received food. Middle-class people did not. |
| From July 1918, all large industries were nationalised. They were brought under government control and given production targets decided in Moscow.<br><br>Workshops employing over ten people were nationalised in 1919. | Increased government control. Workers' Factory Committees were abolished. 'Bourgeois* specialists' (spetsy in Russian) were employed as managers. They did not have to be communists as long as they followed government orders. |
| Money was abolished. The communists believed that money would not be needed in a communist society. | The government paid people in kind*. Money continued to be used in areas that the communists did not fully control – and here inflation ran out of control and prices leapt up. |
| Labour conscription. People were forced to work as directed by the government. There was strict discipline for workers. | Workers' rights were reduced. Strikes became illegal and strikers could be shot. Trade unions were taken over by the Communist Party. |
| In towns and cities, housing belonging to rich people was redistributed, and large houses were split up to house several poor families. | Living space became more equal, and the government had more control over it. Communist Party officials decided who would get a home. These were often spaces in a barracks or shared flat. |
| Public transport in cities was made free of charge. | Workers could get to work more easily. |
| Private markets and trading were banned. | A 'black market'* emerged. People could still buy sought-after goods – such as better-made clothes and shoes, or watches – but they had to do so illegally. |

## Key terms

**Requisition***
Take by force.

**Bourgeois***
Middle-class.

**Payment in kind***
Exchanging goods and services without using money.

**Black market***
Illegal buying and selling.

## Source A

Requisition of flour from rich peasants in a village near Pskov, painted by Ivan Vladimirov a supporter of the government, in 1922.

# The crisis of 1921: from War Communism to the NEP

In 1921, the Communist Party changed direction. In many ways, it was as big a change as getting out of the First World War with the Treaty of Brest-Litovsk. In fact, some Communist Party members called the new direction 'the peasant Brest-Litovsk'. By this, they meant it was something they were forced to do to stay in power, because of peasant opposition to the communists in the countryside. But it wasn't that simple.

## The failure of War Communism

War Communism had to be abandoned because it was an economic disaster and deeply unpopular. By 1921, Russia was facing economic collapse. Peasants were destroying their crops, rather than see them seized by the communists. There were widespread shortages of food and consumer goods. In many country areas there was famine*. It was so bad, that there were even cases of cannibalism – as starving people ate other people.

War Communism had also led to political crisis:

- In Tambov Province there was a huge peasant uprising.
- Lenin and the Communist Party were also shocked by the Kronstadt Mutiny (see pages 60–1).
- Within the Communist Party, a group – called the Workers' Opposition – was unhappy at the way the party ordered workers around, and gave them little involvement in decision-making.

## Key term

**Famine***

Widespread lack of food leading to mass starvation.

- Factory workers – who felt the Communist Party did not represent them, and who were unhappy at falling living standards – organised protests and strikes. (Some had even gone to Kronstadt to get the support of the sailors before the Kronstadt Mutiny.) In response, the Communist Party arrested protestors –

but also increased food rations, to try to stop further protests.

It was clear that something would have to change. If it didn't, the Communist Party might find that it had won the Civil War, only to lose control of the country. It was because of this that War Communism was ended and a new approach was tried: the New Economic Policy (NEP).

## Source B

From a decree of June 1921, on how Red Army soldiers were to treat peasants revolting in Tambov province.

```
1. Citizens who refuse to give their name
are to be executed on the spot.

2. Villages that conceal weapons... are
sentenced to having hostages taken. These
are to be shot if the weapons are not
surrendered.
```

## Source C

Communist poster, dating from 1920, and distributed in the Soviet Union. The caption reads: 'On the ruins of capitalism the brotherhood of peasants and workers marches.'

### Exam-style question, Section A

Give **two** things you can infer from Source C about how the communists wanted to present their relationship with the peasants.

Say what you can infer and give details from the source that tell you this. **4 marks**

### Exam tip

Start by looking at the content of the source. What can you see? Then decide what messages are in the source. These might be obvious, or they might not. You will need to 'decode' the meaning and messages of the source. In your answer, explain what you can infer from the source, and what details of the source are helping you make that inference.

# The New Economic Policy (NEP)

The free market and money were re-introduced. All over Russia, traders hurried to make the most of these new opportunities. These traders became known as 'NEP-men' and 'NEP-women'. Small businesses sprang up across Russia, and it became acceptable for better-off people to employ others again.

The NEP also brought greater freedom for peasants. They welcomed it, and made the most of the new opportunities to trade and improve their standard of living. Seizure of grain was replaced by taxation – at first in farm produce, but, after 1924, paid in cash. Once peasants had paid their taxes, they were free to sell off any leftover grain, and keep the money to spend as they wished.

## Reactions to the NEP

Peasants and traders welcomed the NEP. Even those who did not grow wealthy as a result of it enjoyed the greater freedom. The government liked to pretend that among so-called 'middle peasants' and 'poor peasants' there was support for its previous policies – but virtually all peasants had hated the lack of freedom under War Communism. They hoped that the NEP was how Russia would develop in future.

Many communists, however, were deeply disappointed. Suicides went up among Communist Party members during the time of the NEP. Leading communists – such as Trotsky – opposed what they thought was the re-emergence of capitalism in the communist Soviet Union.

Some workers in the towns were also disappointed: it looked as if the peasants were gaining more from the revolution than they were. Maybe the NEP really was the 'peasant Brest-Litovsk'. For the time being, critics of the NEP had no choice but to accept the situation; but many hoped that the NEP was only a temporary measure.

## Effects of the NEP on the economy, 1921–24

- There was finally growth in agricultural output. Peasants began producing more, because they could now sell it. But agriculture was still very backward with little modern equipment.

- Industry began to grow, but at a very slow rate. Many leading communists thought the NEP would take too long to fully industrialise the Soviet Union and meet the nation's needs.

- The 'Scissors Crisis'. By the middle of 1923, there were fewer food shortages and prices of agricultural products were falling. This was because peasants were producing more grain. However, prices for factory-made goods were going up. This was because industry was growing slowly. Manufactured goods were scarce and cost more to buy. To the communists it seemed clear that industry was not going to expand quickly enough under the NEP. Trotsky called this the 'Scissors Crisis'.

- Society became more unequal, as some people did better out of the NEP than others. Wealthier peasants (the kulaks) became targets for Communist Party complaints, as did the traders known as 'NEP-men' and 'NEP-women'.

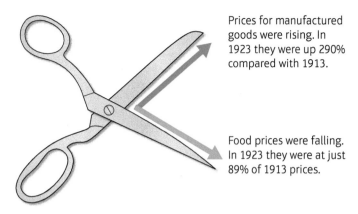

Prices for manufactured goods were rising. In 1923 they were up 290% compared with 1913.

Food prices were falling. In 1923 they were at just 89% of 1913 prices.

**Figure 2.6** The Scissors Crisis, 1923.

- Trade with foreign countries remained below the level that it had been in 1913. The Soviet Union was slipping behind the economic growth of neighbouring (non-communist) countries.

## How different was the NEP from War Communism?

In many ways, NEP was very different from the policy of War Communism. But, in other ways, things did not change much. The government kept control of what they called the 'Commanding Heights': the banks and major industries, like steel and coal. The government had no intention of losing control of the whole of the economy. And there was no political relaxation: Russia remained a one-party state, and trade unions remained under the control of the Communist Party.

### Source D

From a speech made by Lenin to Communist Party members at the 10th Party Congress in March 1921.

The peasant must do a bit of starving so as to relieve the factories and towns from complete starvation. On the level of the state in general this is an entirely understandable thing, but we're not counting on the exhausted, destitute peasant-owner understanding it. And we know you can't manage without compulsion...

## Source E

From *The Tax in Kind*, a pamphlet written by Lenin to explain why the NEP was being introduced. It was published in 1921.

We were forced to resort to 'war communism' by war and ruin. It was a temporary measure... it [NEP] is necessary, to a certain extent, to help to restore small industry... The proletarian regime [though] is in no danger as long as the proletariat firmly holds power in its hands, as long as it firmly holds transport and large-scale industry.

## Activities ?

1  Why did the communists introduce War Communism? Use Source E to help you answer this question, along with other information from this section. If Source E gives the 'official' reason, do you think there was another 'real' reason?

2  List the main features of War Communism and the NEP.

3  How different was the NEP from War Communism? With a partner compare your lists, and identify what changed and what stayed the same, before deciding how different the NEP was.

# Dealing with the crisis of 1921: the 10th Party Congress

At the 10th Party Congress, Lenin was able to deal with many aspects of the crises threatening the power of the Communist Party. He knew that, without action, opposition to government policy would undermine communist rule. The following changes helped him consolidate the communist hold on power, and reduce opposition to his leadership:

- The move from War Communism to the NEP was agreed.
- Factionalism* was banned. This meant that Communist Party members were not allowed to criticise the centralised party control of power. From this time onwards, once the Communist Party had made a decision, all members were expected to support it. If they carried on criticising it, or arguing for a different policy, then they would be condemned as 'factionalists' and could be expelled from the party. This included the Workers' Opposition, who wanted workers to have more say in how their factories were run, and to allow trade unions more involvement in decision making.
- Many of the party's members were expelled because they were regarded as not being committed enough communists, or they were from the 'wrong' social class. In country areas, about 44% of Communist Party members from peasant backgrounds were expelled from the party.

## Key term

**Factionalism***

Being part of a group that stands out against what others (usually those in authority) think.

## The communists and social change
### Impact of communist policies on women

### Interpretation 1

From *The Russian Revolution from Lenin to Stalin, 1917–1929*, by E.H. Carr, published in 1979.

*The bitterness of the controversy [the move to the NEP and the defeat of the Workers' Opposition] shocked the party, and left its mark on the congress. Lenin spoke of the "fever" which had shaken the party and of "the luxury of discussions" and "disputes" which the party could ill afford. The congress adopted a special resolution... Once a decision had been taken, unconditional obedience to it was obligatory. Infringement of this rule could lead to expulsion from the party... These provisions, designed to ensure loyalty and uniformity of opinion in the party, seemed necessary and reasonable at the time.*

### Activity ?

Imagine a conversation between two communists at the 10th Party Congress and write a dialogue. One supports Lenin: basing your points on Interpretation 1, explain why the restrictions on discussions in the party are necessary. The other is a member of the Workers' Opposition: in their reply, include reasons why they are not happy with the way that the Communist Party is developing.

**1917**
Women declared equal with men.
Divorce is made easier. 'Postcard divorces' costing three rubles are introduced. The divorced partner hears the news through the post.
Non-religious marriage introduced.

**1919**
New women's organisation, the Zhenotdel, set up to increase freedom and influence of women. Its leader is Alexandra Kollontai. Lenin disapproved of Kollontai's beliefs in 'sexual freedom' and does not like her support for the Workers' Opposition.

**1920**
Abortion is made legal.
More women learn to read and write thanks to Civil War literacy campaigns.

**1923**
Alexandra Kollontai becomes world's first female ambassador, serving in Norway.

**1926**
Women can legally own property in a relationship – previously it belonged to their husbands.

**Figure 2.7** Impact of communist policies on women.

## Source F

Revolutionary poster from the 1920s, celebrating the contribution of women to the Soviet Union.

## The impact of the NEP on women

NEP may have been popular with peasants but, under it, women's rights declined. Cutbacks in government spending led to a decline in the number of crèches provided in factories, and this limited job opportunities for women. At the same time, many women were still expected to do all the domestic chores on top of work. There is also evidence that some male members of the government – while officially in favour of women's rights – did not regard it as a priority; and few women were promoted to top jobs in the Communist Party. As a consequence, progress on women's rights slowed down in the second half of the 1920s. The revolution had brought only a limited equality for women in their everyday lives.

## Timeline

### Impact of communism on society, 1917–25

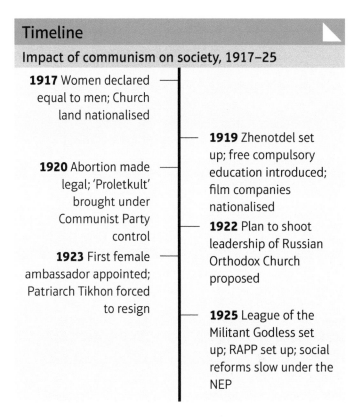

**1917** Women declared equal to men; Church land nationalised

**1919** Zhenotdel set up; free compulsory education introduced; film companies nationalised

**1920** Abortion made legal; 'Proletkult' brought under Communist Party control

**1922** Plan to shoot leadership of Russian Orthodox Church proposed

**1923** First female ambassador appointed; Patriarch Tikhon forced to resign

**1925** League of the Militant Godless set up; RAPP set up; social reforms slow under the NEP

## Impact of communist policies on education

Free compulsory education, to the age of 17, was established in 1919. Pre-school education was provided in many factories. There was also a major literacy drive within the Red Army. In country areas, peasants were encouraged to learn to read and write. By 1926, about 58% of the population was literate, which was much greater than before the revolution. Anatoly Lunacharsky was made the first Soviet People's Commissar of Education, responsible for education and culture.

However, as late as 1927 – despite the efforts of the Communist Party – only 5% of teachers were party members; and it was not until the 1930s that education was completely reorganised along communist lines. Until then, it was still possible to find textbooks in schools that dated from the time of the tsar. Teachers were not trusted, so their authority was limited by banning homework and corporal punishment* – and their pay rate was set below that of a factory worker.

## Key term

**Corporal punishment***
Physical punishment such as slapping and caning.

# Impact of communist policies on culture

The communists believed in the propaganda power of art and education. In the early 1920s, they set up a government department known as Agitprop – short for Agitation and Propaganda Section of the Central Committee Secretariat of the Communist Party. Its job was to make sure that education and mass communication supported the Communist Party.

## Art

During the 1920s, the Communist Party encouraged what they called 'Proletarian culture'. This meant art which supported the revolution and put workers centre-stage. At this time, however, there was no clear official idea of what this would look like.

For some *avant garde** artists the revolution brought new freedom to paint in abstract* and geometric* designs. 'Futurists' aimed to break with the past and wanted non-representational art that communicated ideas about modern life and industry. Lenin, however, liked more traditional art and a realistic style.

As a result, the 1920s in the Soviet Union was a time of artistic variety and creativity – but there were restrictions too. For example, in 1920, a movement called Proletkult – which had started in 1917 to encourage worker involvement in experimental art – was brought under Communist Party control.

## Religion

The communists were atheists* and wanted to get rid of all religion. To start with, though, they promised more freedom for Jews and Muslims, who had experienced discrimination (often very violent, in the case of Jews) under the tsars.

### Key terms

**Avant garde***

New and experimental ideas.

**Abstract***

Art that does not resemble reality.

**Geometric***

Using regular lines and mathematical shapes.

**Atheist***

A person who believes that there is no God.

The communists particularly wanted to reduce the influence of the Orthodox Church, which had closely supported the tsar and often supported the Whites during the Civil War. The communists saw the Orthodox Church as a counter-revolutionary organisation.

### Source G

A recent photograph of Kazan Cathedral, Moscow. The cathedral was rebuilt in 1993 as an exact replica of the original building, which was destroyed on Stalin's orders in 1936.

In 1917, Church land had been seized. The Church also lost its control over education. In 1922, Lenin increased persecution of the Orthodox Church. Many priests were shot, and Church property and valuables were confiscated by force. In 1923, the leader of the Orthodox Church, Patriarch Tikhon, was forced to resign, and this weakened the leadership of the Church. In 1925, the communists set up a group called the League of the Militant Godless to spread anti-religious propaganda. Anti-religious museums were also set up, often in former churches. The communists hoped that, over time, religion would die out. They were wrong.

### Activity ?

Create a revision guide to the impact of the Communist Party on society in the Soviet Union using the headings: 'Women', 'Education', 'Culture', and Religion'. Gather information from this chapter showing: what the communists felt about each of these things; what changed under communism; how much things changed under communism.

## Literature

Censorship by a government department – called Glavit – ensured that books carried messages that the communists approved of. Like artists, many writers welcomed the revolution as a bringer of freedom. From the mid-1920s, though, the communists brought writers under tighter control. From 1925, this control was carried out by the Russian Association of Proletarian Writers (RAPP), which promoted a style of novel called 'socialist realism' featuring stories of heroic communists.

## Film and music

Film was overseen by a special section of the Ministry of Education; and all film companies were nationalised in 1919. Many communist films were made during the Civil War; and in the 1920s propaganda films were shown in factories, free of charge. Some of these films found ground-breaking ways of making the stories they told more dramatic and engaging. One of the most famous is *October*, directed by Eisenstein, which tells the story of the 1917 revolution.

Classical music and ballet went out of fashion because they were associated with the tsarist nobility. Composers who stayed in Russia tended to support the new political ideas. Many others left Russia. The Russian Association of Proletarian Musicians (RAPM) brought political control to music. New styles of music tried to imitate work, or the military – with sounds like machinery and factory sirens.

---

**THINKING HISTORICALLY** ▸ **Interpretations (2b)**

### The importance of perspective

What we notice when we look at a historical source is shaped by our interests, questions and concepts. Historians are individuals too – and what they 'see' is shaped by what they are interested in, and what they see as important. Historians also sometimes use different methods of investigating, and will make sense of sources in different ways.

Study Source G and the information about it.

The photo shows 'traces' of the past (e.g. the site where this church was once destroyed and then rebuilt). Traces can be interpreted in many ways, depending on the questions asked, and the interests and concepts that we bring to them.

1 Look closely at the image and the accompanying text. Discuss the following questions with a partner and write down your ideas.

   a What might an architectural historian notice about the picture? What story would they tell about change and continuity?

   b What might a cultural historian, with an interest in how people practise religion, notice about the picture? What story might they tell about change and continuity?

   c Explain how the two stories differ and why.

2 Sometimes historians look at history in great depth, but sometimes they are interested in getting more of an overview of what happened. Look at the image again.

   a How would a historian interested in religious architecture in the whole of Europe study this building? How much detail would they go into, and what might they compare it to?

   b How would a historian interested in the religious buildings of Russia study this building? How much detail would they go into, and what might they compare it to?

   c Explain how the scale that a historian is thinking about affects how they look at sources.

3 Answer the following question in a paragraph of your own: How important are the interests, questions and concepts that historians bring to their study of the past in shaping their interpretations?

## Summary

- War Communism was introduced to try to control the Russian economy.
- When War Communism failed, it was replaced by the NEP in 1921.
- Despite the change to the NEP, there was no political relaxation.
- The communists introduced many changes that affected all aspects of Russian society and culture.

## Checkpoint

### Strengthen

**S1** Write a short historical-dictionary definition of 'War Communism'.

**S2** Write a short historical-dictionary definition of the 'New Economic Policy'.

**S3** Choose one of the following, and explain how communist rule changed it: life for women, education, art, literature, religion.

### Challenge

**C1** 'War Communism was not really a temporary measure. The communists only said this after it had failed.' What do you think? Does the evidence support this interpretation?

**C2** How different was the NEP to War Communism?

**C3** To what extent did communist rule really change women's lives?

How confident are you about your answers to these questions? To improve your answers, form a small group to compare answers, then get your teacher to check the ideas that you have produced.

# Recap: The Bolsheviks in power 1917–24

## Recall quiz

1 What was the name of the parliament that briefly met in January 1918?

2 Which political party won the most seats in it?

3 What was the name of the treaty by which Russia left the First World War?

4 What colour was used to describe the Bolshevik armies in the Civil War?

5 Who was Commissar for War during the Civil War?

6 What name is used to describe the running of the economy in the Civil War?

7 Sailors from which naval base revolted in 1921?

8 What does NEP stand for?

9 What was the Russian name for the organisation designed to increase the freedom and influence of women?

10 What was a postcard divorce?

## Activity ?

How much did Russia change between 1917 and 1924? Working together in small groups, start by:

- reviewing what Russia was like at the start of Chapter 1
- reviewing how it changed during 1917 (again, recap from Chapter 1)
- reviewing this chapter.

Note all the changes you notice under these headings:

- Political
- Economic
- Social
- Military

How much did the country change in each area? How much did it change overall?

## Activities ?

1 Write a short paragraph explaining how government of Russia was organised under Lenin? Which different bodies within government and the party existed, and what were their roles?

2 How did the Bolshevik/Communist Party's conduct of warfare compare with that of the tsar and the Provisional Government?

3 How successfully did the Bolsheviks/communists impose their rule on Russia between the October Revolution in 1917 and the change to the New Economic Policy in 1921?

# 03 | Stalin's rise to power and dictatorship, 1924–41

Lenin became seriously ill in 1922 – and died in January 1924. A power struggle then took place in the Soviet Union over who would succeed him as leader.

By 1929, Stalin had defeated all his rivals to become leader of the Communist Party – and the country. However, he did not feel that he was securely in power. Between 1936 and 1938, he launched a series of bloody purges – sometimes called the 'Great Terror' – which destroyed all rivals and potential rivals, aimed to root out opposition to the government and its plans, and killed millions – as the whole country was terrorised into unquestioning obedience to his rule.

Even after the worst of the terror subsided, the Soviet Union remained under the brutal control of the secret police who upheld Stalin's dictatorship. At the same time, the Communist Party increased its control of the media, art, culture, religion and education – through ruthless censorship and constant propaganda – as it attempted to dominate the minds and lives of all citizens of the Soviet Union.

As part of this process, a 'cult of Stalin' was developed, which attempted to put Stalin at the centre of life – presenting him as Lenin's most loyal disciple, who had fulfilled all Lenin's plans for building a revolutionary communist state.

## Learning outcomes

By the end of this chapter you will:

- know how Stalin won the power struggle in the 1920s, following the death of Lenin
- understand why the purges of the 1930s (the Great Terror) happened, and know about their effects on the country
- be able to explain how Stalin and the Communist Party used propaganda and censorship to reinforce his dictatorship
- know why the cult of Stalin was introduced.

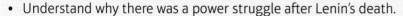

## Learning outcomes

- Understand why there was a power struggle after Lenin's death.
- Know about the different people who could potentially have become leader after Lenin.
- Understand how Stalin defeated his rivals to become leader.

## Replacing Lenin: complications

Lenin fell ill – suffering a series of strokes – in 1922 and 1923 – and eventually died in January 1924. Throughout much of 1923, he was so ill that he played no real part in government. During this time, a struggle started among senior communists for leadership of the Communist Party, and rule over the Soviet Union. By 1928, this struggle had been won by Stalin. Looking back from the present day, it can seem that he was always going to win – but this was certainly not the case. At the time when Lenin died, few people would have predicted that Stalin would become the 'new Lenin'.

The task of replacing Lenin was made more complicated by the fact that he didn't hold one specific leadership job. While Lenin had key roles in government (as chairman of Sovnarkom) and chaired meetings of the party's Politburo, there was no single job that summed up his role. He controlled power as much through the force of his personality, as by the positions that he held. So, when he died, it was not just a matter of someone else stepping into a vacant position.

Stalin, for example, was the General Secretary of the Communist Party (responsible for membership, allocation of jobs and organisation of the party), a job that Lenin never held – though, after Stalin, all leaders of the Soviet Union held this job. But in 1924, few people realised just how powerful a job it was – in fact, it seemed very dull and boring.

The matter was made even more uncertain by the fact that Lenin had left a 'testament'* in which he criticised all the other leading communists – but most of all Stalin. Just before he died, Lenin had broken off relations with Stalin, because Stalin had been rude to Lenin's wife, Krupskaya.

### Source A

The criticisms of leading communists in Lenin's testament, written in December 1922.

Comrade **Stalin** has unlimited authority concentrated in his hands, and I am not sure whether he will always be capable of using that authority with sufficient caution... **Stalin** is too rude.... That is why I suggest the comrades think about a way of removing **Stalin** from that post and appointing another man... more tolerant, more loyal, more polite, and more considerate to the comrades...

Comrade **Trotsky**, on the other hand, is personally perhaps the most capable man in the present Central Committee, but he has displayed excessive self-assurance and shown excessive preoccupation with the purely administrative side of the work...

I shall just recall that the October episode with **Zinoviev and Kamenev** [they had opposed seizing power in the October Revolution of 1917] was, of course, no accident, but neither can the blame for it be laid upon them personally, any more than non-Bolshevism can upon **Trotsky**.

**Bukharin** is rightly considered the favourite of the whole Party, but his theoretical views can be classified as fully Marxist only with the greatest reserve.

### Key term

**Testament***

A written document detailing a person's wishes for what should happen after they die.

Why did Lenin criticise them all? Possibly he thought that none of them, on their own, was capable of replacing him as leader – and, instead, he wanted them all to work together.

He did not see Trotsky as his successor, as some modern writers suggest. At the end of his life, though, Lenin feared Stalin – and for Stalin, Lenin's testament was a great embarrassment.

---

**Exam-style question, Section A**

Give **two** things you can infer from Source A about Lenin's attitude towards his fellow leaders.

Say what you can infer and give details from the source that tell you this.                    **4 marks**

---

**Exam tip**

Don't just copy from the source. Think about what it tells you about Lenin's attitude – consider the meaning of the words and the outlook behind them. Then explain what the source tells you. Don't forget to state explicitly what it is in the source that made you think this.

---

# The rivals for power

## Stalin

### Strengths

- He was general secretary of the Communist Party. This gave him tremendous power, through appointing supporters to key jobs in the party, and through organising the congresses of the Communist Party. He was also in charge of encouraging more workers to join the party after Lenin's death: the 'Lenin Enrolment'. These poorly educated new members were very loyal to Stalin as the man who had allowed them into the party.
- He appeared to be a moderate in how he dealt with rivals – as he was careful not to get angry.
- He seemed to be in the 'centre' of the party, and not too extreme in the way that he wanted things to develop in the party and the Soviet Union.
- He seemed patriotic, as he believed in 'Socialism in One Country' – the belief that the Soviet Union could become a communist country even if the revolution did not spread to other countries.

### Weaknesses

- He had been seriously criticised in Lenin's Testament.
- He had a reputation for being rather boring. Party comrades jokingly called him 'the grey blur' and 'Comrade Card Index' (a way of storing records before the use of modern computers).

## Trotsky

### Strengths

- He was a brilliant speaker.
- He had worked closely with Lenin.
- He helped the Communist Party win the Civil War.

### Weaknesses

- He was considered arrogant. Ordering people about had worked well in the Civil War – when tough action was needed – but in peacetime people resented it.
- He did not join the party until 1917, so did not have a strong network of friends and supporters like his rivals. Lenin's support had helped him overcome this – but after Lenin's death, this support was gone.
- His belief in 'Permanent Revolution' looked unpatriotic – his view was that communism could only succeed if it spread to other countries.
- He did not offer Russia the chance to pause and organise itself – as he wanted rapid industrialisation to replace the NEP.

## Zinoviev and Kamenev

### Strengths

- These two communists worked closely together.
- They were the party bosses in Petrograd (renamed Leningrad in 1924) and Moscow.
- Zinoviev had a reputation as an insightful communist thinker and a rousing speaker.

### Weaknesses

- They had opposed Lenin's plans for the October Revolution which hung over them as a terrible criticism.

## Bukharin

### Strengths

- A brilliant thinker and political writer.
- Personally very popular in the party.

## Weaknesses

- He lacked experience.
- After initially opposing the NEP, he had come to support it as a way of steadily building up the Soviet Union's economy towards industrialisation. This was not a popular position in the Communist Party.

### Extend your knowledge

**The quiet man**

During the bitter disagreements of 1924 and 1925, it was said, that at meetings of the Central Committee of the Communist Party, Stalin would shake hands with Trotsky, but Zinoviev would not. Stalin was skilful at making himself appear moderate and above squabbles. He also kept his thoughts to himself, whereas others expressed opinions openly and loudly. A fellow communist once remarked that Stalin spoke little, in a country where everybody else said too much.

### Activities ?

1 Reread Source A. List the weaknesses of Stalin, Trotsky, Zinoviev and Kamenev, and Bukharin – according to Lenin.

2 Discuss the weaknesses with a partner. Decide whose weakness (according to Lenin) was most serious and write a short paragraph to explain why.

3 Using Source A, along with the other information about the strengths and weaknesses of the rivals for power, explain why Stalin was in a strong position even before Lenin died in 1924.

## The aftermath of Lenin's death

After Lenin's death, Stalin quickly made two smart moves: he supressed Lenin's testament and organised Lenin's funeral.

The other communist leaders agreed that the testament should not be published – because it criticised them too – so few learned about Lenin's fears regarding Stalin.

In organising Lenin's funeral, Stalin appeared close to Lenin and a leading figure. This was the start of the cult of Lenin*. Stalin was always very careful to present himself as Lenin's loyal follower, and simply striving to put Leninism* into practice. In 1924, the name of the city of Petrograd was even changed to 'Leningrad'.

Trotsky was ill and did not attend Lenin's funeral. Later he claimed that Stalin had given him the wrong date, which is hard to believe. It looks more as if Trotsky simply didn't know how to compete with his rivals, who had swiftly united against him. He seemed out of his depth.

### Key terms

**Cult of Lenin***

Treating Lenin and his ideas with great reverence and devotion.

**Leninism***

The form of communism, adapted by Lenin for Russia and its conditions.

### Source B

A photograph of Lenin's funeral. Stalin is at the front, on the left, carrying the coffin.

# Stalin eliminates the opposition: the power struggle

## Timeline

**The power struggle, 1924–29**

**1924** Death of Lenin

**1925** Trotsky loses job as Commissar for War

**1926** United Opposition is formed

**1927** United Opposition defeated; Zinoviev, Kamenev and Trotsky expelled from Communist Party

**1929** Bukharin expelled from the Politburo; Trotsky expelled from the USSR; Stalin wins power struggle

Stalin eventually emerged as the leader of the Soviet Union by making a series of political moves – or 'steps to power'. Each step saw him beat at least one of his rivals and improve his own position.

Looking back on Stalin's success, it can almost look as if he had a plan – as step-by-step he advanced to power. However, there is no evidence to suggest there was a plan; and it is unrealistic to imagine that there could have been one – as he could not possibly have predicted the actions and mistakes made by his rivals.

Rather than a plan, what Stalin had was the ability to make the most of any situation. He was calculating and quick to seize an opportunity. He was also prepared to change his position on issues in order to put his opponents at a disadvantage. He was also prepared to switch sides to isolate his rivals – and never took all of them on at one time.

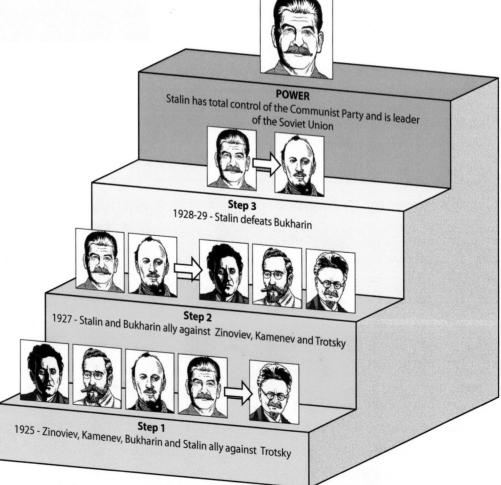

**POWER**
Stalin has total control of the Communist Party and is leader of the Soviet Union

**Step 3**
1928-29 - Stalin defeats Bukharin

**Step 2**
1927 - Stalin and Bukharin ally against Zinoviev, Kamenev and Trotsky

**Step 1**
1925 - Zinoviev, Kamenev, Bukharin and Stalin ally against Trotsky

**Figure 3.1** Stalin's key steps in eliminating the opposition.

## Step 1: defeating Trotsky and the 'Left Communists'

After Lenin's death, Trotsky was seen as the real danger by Zinoviev, Kamenev and Bukharin – who were ready to work with Stalin in order to isolate Trotsky. Going along with them was a successful tactic* on Stalin's part. Trotsky made things worse for himself by criticising the lack of democracy in the party. This sounded like an attack on Lenin's party. It was also unpopular with those who had found jobs in the party. It was a poor tactic by Trotsky.

There were also disagreements over strategy*. Trotsky and the 'Left Communists' wanted Permanent Revolution, rapid industrialisation, and an end to the NEP. 'Right Communists' were prepared to put up with the NEP for longer, in order to build a foundation for industrialisation. This began to look like a difference over ideology* – but it wasn't really, as both sides wanted to industrialise as soon as possible.

At the Party Congress in 1925, Stalin's control of the party organisation, and Zinoviev and Kamenev's control of the party in Leningrad and Moscow, meant that all the votes went their way. Trotsky lost his job as Commissar for War and some tried to expel him from the party. This was blocked by the 'moderate' Stalin.

## Step 2: defeating the 'United Opposition'

In terms of their ideology, Zinoviev and Kamenev were actually in agreement with Trotsky. They wanted an end to the NEP and the start of rapid industrialisation. They just disagreed with his attacks on how the party was run. But they also disagreed with Bukharin, who had become a supporter of the NEP.

Unable to get support in a party dominated by Stalin, they then adopted tactics which proved a major mistake. They formed the 'United Opposition' with Trotsky and criticised the way the party was running the economy. This was an error. For a start, it looked bizarre that they were now allies with their former enemy, Trotsky. Also, their criticisms of party policies allowed Stalin to accuse them of being 'factionalists' – something outlawed by Lenin at the 10th Party Congress in 1921. Zinoviev and Kamenev were sacked from all their jobs. In 1927, they and Trotsky were expelled from the party. Zinoviev and Kamenev later admitted they were 'wrong' and were allowed back in. Trotsky refused to admit he was wrong, and was expelled from the Soviet Union in 1929.

### Key terms

**Tactic***
Dealing with issues day-to-day. Tactics might change, depending on circumstances.

**Strategy***
A person's overall goals – what they are working to achieve.

**Ideology***
The beliefs that a person holds.

### Extend your knowledge

**Trotsky in exile**

Trotsky was first sent into internal exile in Kazakhstan in 1928, before being exiled from the Soviet Union in 1929. He then lived in Turkey, France, Norway and eventually Mexico. In exile, he wrote books condemning the way that Stalin was ruling the Soviet Union. In August 1940, he was murdered – with a mountaineer's ice-axe – by an agent sent by Stalin.

## Step 3: defeating Bukharin and the 'Right Communists'

In his ideology, and his strategy, Stalin was identical to Trotsky, Zinoviev and Kamenev when it came to industrialising the Soviet Union. He believed in doing it quickly. But he had followed the tactic of siding with Bukharin as a way of isolating his opponents. Now it only remained to dispose of Bukharin. This was not difficult: Bukharin lacked support in the party; could not control the votes at party congresses, like Stalin could; and was in favour of the unpopular policy of the NEP.

Stalin made his move in the winter of 1927–28. Poor relations between the Soviet Union and western countries made many in the Soviet Union fearful of war at this time; and, on top of that, there had been a poor harvest in 1927. In order to win a war, the Soviet Union would have to build up its industrial strength quickly; and food supplies needed to be controlled, both to feed the cities, and to sell abroad to pay for industrialisation. Stalin visited Siberia and ordered the police to seize grain from peasants who were accused of hoarding it, as they had been during the Civil War. This use of force became known as 'the Urals-Siberia method'. It broke all the rules of the NEP.

---

**THINKING HISTORICALLY** **Interpretations (2a)**

### The importance of selection

Historians do not aim to tell us about the whole past – there is just too much of it. They need to choose which aspects of the past to investigate – and which details are most important to examine. For example, an overview history of the stages by which Stalin won the power struggle might not explore the detail of the personal relationships between the rivals; whereas an examination of the workings of the Central Committee of the Communist Party might look in more depth at the way these leaders interacted and the impact of this on events.

The power struggle in the Soviet Union – some key information

| A) Stalin was a Georgian, not a Russian. | B) Stalin was made General Secretary under Lenin. | C) Lenin had a series of strokes in 1922 and 1923. | D) Stalin and Lenin's wife had a huge argument. |
|---|---|---|---|
| E) Lenin wrote a testament which criticised Stalin. | F) Trotsky suffered from illnesses in 1923–24 and often did not perform well. | G) After Lenin's death the testament was not published. | H) Stalin was always polite to Trotsky at Central Committee meetings. |
| I) Trotsky lost his job as Commissar for War in 1925. | J) Zinoviev, Kamenev and Trotsky formed the United Opposition. | K) In 1927 Zinoviev, Kamenev and Trotsky were expelled from the party. | L) Bukharin was expelled from his top jobs and from the Politburo in 1929. Stalin had won. |

To study history, historians have to focus on a particular question to investigate. Which of the above pieces of information would be best suited for investigating the following issues? Write out each of the four questions below, and then choose up to four pieces of information from the table for each.

1   The stages by which Stalin won the power struggle.

2   The influence of Lenin on the power struggle.

3   The impact of personal relationships on how the power struggle developed.

4   The impact of chance on historical events.

With a partner, discuss the following questions and write down your thoughts:

5   Why is it important to be selective about the information that you put in your historical writing?

6   How important are the questions the historian asks in deciding what information is included in their writing?

Then, during 1929, Stalin called for the collectivisation* of agriculture and the launch of Five-Year Plans (see Chapter 4) to industrialise the Soviet Union rapidly. Bukharin was unable to stop this, as Stalin controlled the party organisation. Bukharin and his allies (the 'Right Communists') were condemned as the 'Right Deviation'. Stalin used the word 'deviation' to suggest they were not real communists.

In desperation, secretly Bukharin began to discuss with Kamenev how Stalin might be stopped. News of these meetings leaked out, and Bukharin was expelled from his top jobs, and from the Politburo in 1929. Stalin had finally triumphed over all his rivals.

## Key term

**Collectivisation***
The taking over of peasant farms by the state in the early 1930s.

## Summary

- Lenin's lengthy illness meant that the power struggle started even before he died in 1924.
- At the end of his life, Lenin feared Stalin – but criticised all the rivals for power in his testament.
- Stalin's job as General Secretary gave him great advantages in the power struggle.
- Stalin's victory was not inevitable: he was assisted by his job, his use of clever tactics, and the mistakes of his rivals.

## Checkpoint

### Strengthen

**S1** For each of the rivals, create a spidergram, showing their strengths in one colour, and their weaknesses in another.

**S2** Try to sum up, in one sentence, how Stalin's job assisted him to win the power struggle.

### Challenge

**C1** How big a mistake do you think Lenin made in criticising all the other leaders?

**C2** Given his success in the Civil War, why was Trotsky so easily defeated in the power struggle?

**C3** Put together a debate around the point of view: 'Stalin was always going to win the power struggle'. In one small group make the case for this, while another small group makes the case against. Make your presentation to each other and question each other. Then take a secret vote on which argument you are most persuaded by. It might not be your own.

How confident do you feel about your answers to these questions? Reread this section, making notes as you go, then try answering the questions again.

# 3.2 The use of terror in the 1930s

## Learning outcomes

- Understand why Stalin carried out a series of 'purges' in the 1930s.
- Know about the main events of the purges – including show trials.
- Know the main features of the 'Gulag' prison camp system.

## Purges and the use of terror in the Soviet Union

When a government uses mass arrests, imprisonment and force and violence, to destroy real or imagined enemies and to terrify the population – so that it's incapable of opposing the government – we call this the use of 'terror'. When Stalin did this – in the 1930s – he was building on earlier foundations.

## Timeline

### The purges of the 1930s

**1931** Ex-Mensheviks shot as 'wreckers'

**1932** Stalin fails to persuade the Politburo to have Ryutin shot

**1934** Murder of Kirov

**1936** Explosions (mining accidents) at the Kemerovo coal mines

Stalin informs the NKVD they are four years behind in their search for 'enemies'

First show trials: Zinoviev and Kamenev shot

**1937** Start of the *Yezhovschina* ('Time of Yezhov')

Operational Order 00447 issued to the NKVD – start of mass arrests

Purge of the military

**1938** Last great show trial: Bukharin shot

Yezhov arrested (and later shot) – end of the 'Time of Yezhov'

**1939** By this time, about seven million people are imprisoned in labour camps

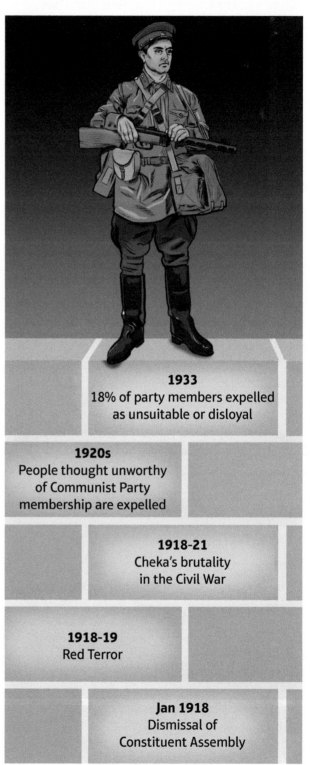

**1933** 18% of party members expelled as unsuitable or disloyal

**1920s** People thought unworthy of Communist Party membership are expelled

**1918-21** Cheka's brutality in the Civil War

**1918-19** Red Terror

**Jan 1918** Dismissal of Constituent Assembly

**Figure 3.2** The foundations of Stalin's use of terror.

The use of terror had started under Lenin, and there were both similarities and differences in Lenin and Stalin's use of terror.

84

## Interpretation 1

From *Lenin, Life and Legacy*, by D. Volkogonov, published in 1994.

*Lenin was willing to commit appallingly cruel acts in the name of the revolution. Although he was not personally vindictive, like Stalin, he did believe that the revolution would fail if the millstones of the dictatorship ceased to grind for a moment.*

## Interpretation 2

From *A People's Tragedy*, by O. Figes, published in 1996.

*On the one hand it seems clear that the basic elements of the Stalinist regime – the one-party state, the system of terror and the cult of the personality – were all in place by 1924… On the other hand, there were fundamental differences between Lenin's regime and that of Stalin. Fewer people were murdered for a start. And, despite the ban on factions, the party still made room for comradely debate. Trotsky and Bukharin argued passionately with each other about the strategy of the NEP… but these were still intellectual debates… despite their differences, neither would have dreamt of using these debates as a pretext [reason] to murder one another, or to send their opponents to Siberia. Only Stalin was capable of this.*

## The role of the secret police

In 1934, the secret police (the OGPU) was reorganised and changed its initials to NKVD. Its work remained the same though: destroying anyone considered to be an enemy of communist rule. The work of the secret police included: intimidating people; arresting people; forcing confessions from people who had been arrested through repeated interrogation (the 'conveyor system'); running prisons; and executing people.

After 1935, three-man teams of NKVD officers (*troikas*) decided people's guilt and punishment. Under Article 58 of the Criminal Code, many people were arrested for betraying the Soviet Union as 'enemies of the people'. In reality many had done things as innocent as:

- stamp-collecting (a link to foreign countries)
- speaking to foreigners
- failing to cut photos of Trotsky from textbooks

- accidentally scribbling on a photo of Stalin in a newspaper
- failing to meet factory production targets.

Others were arrested for no reason at all – the NKVD was set quotas for the number of arrests to make in their area, and if these had not been met, they simply went around arresting more people!

## Reasons behind the purges

The Russian words '*zachem*' ('why') and '*za chto*' ('what for') were often scratched on the walls of prison cells in the 1930s by desperate and confused prisoners. They were fair questions. Why did the purges – also known as the Great Terror – happen?

### To cover up problems in the economy

There were accidents in poorly run mines (such as explosions in the Kemerovo mines in 1936) but the government made it seem like 'enemies' were causing these accidents. Experts, and others, were blamed for deliberately causing problems in the mines and factories – then they were shot. People were shot as a warning to others, and to show how important it was to meet targets. Factory managers often resented, and tried to discourage, super-keen workers called Stakhanovites* (see Section 4.2). These managers soon found themselves in the firing line, as they were blamed for getting in the way of moving the economy forward quickly.

### Key term

**Stakhanovite***

An enthusiastic worker who gained rewards by producing more than other workers.

### To control peasants and workers better

Many workers in the Soviet Union were not used to factory discipline and drifted from job to job. Some of them used false papers. Some people also lied about their background to try to 'reinvent themselves', in order to survive in the communist Soviet Union. For example, Kulaks released from prison, and peasants escaping a famine caused by collectivisation in the Ukraine, fled to the growing cities to try to start a new life. Executions were used to remove any people who were not trusted by the state.

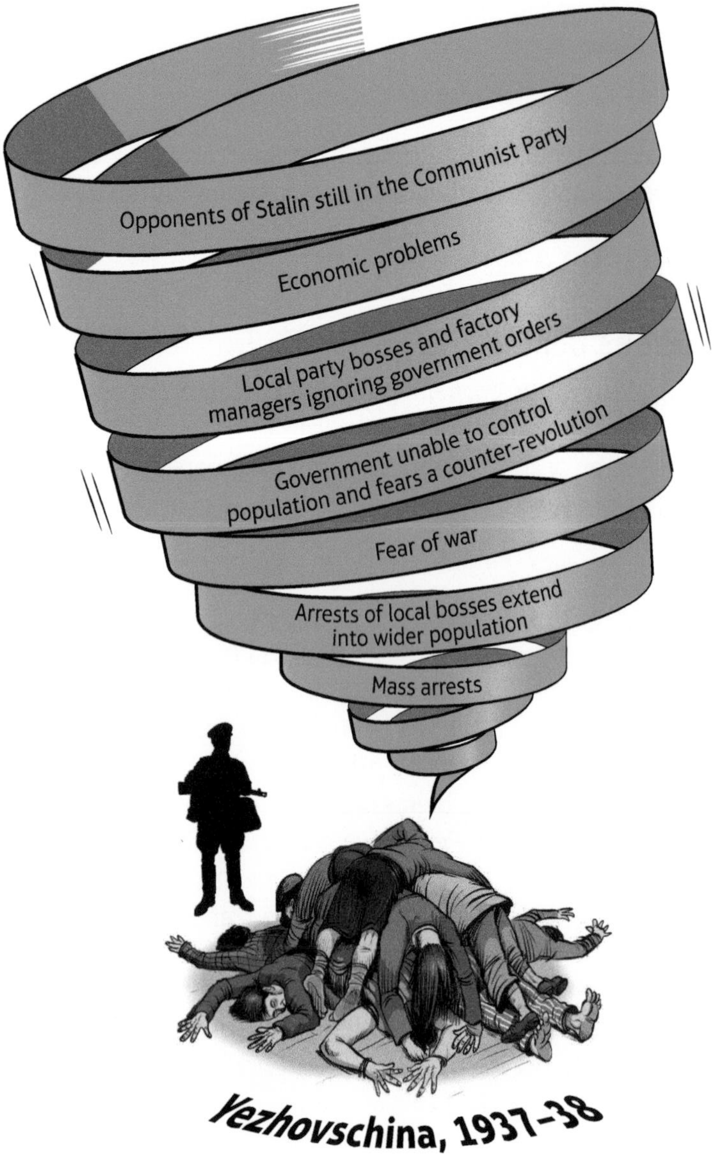
Opponents of Stalin still in the Communist Party
Economic problems
Local party bosses and factory managers ignoring government orders
Government unable to control population and fears a counter-revolution
Fear of war
Arrests of local bosses extend into wider population
Mass arrests
Yezhovschina, 1937–38

**Figure 3.3** The spiral of causes that led to the purges and the *Yezhovschina* in 1937–38.

### *To remove old rivals within the Communist Party*

Although Stalin had won the power struggle, he did not feel secure. Zinoviev, Kamenev, Bukharin, and their allies, were still in the Communist Party. As problems increased in agriculture and industry, other leading communists became critical of Stalin. 'Old Bolsheviks' resented the one-man rule of Stalin. In 1932, Stalin wanted one of these – Ryutin – shot, but could not persuade the Politburo to kill a leading communist. This weakness clearly angered Stalin, and left him feeling more insecure – so he wanted his rivals dead. As a result, many of those who had been close associates of Lenin – and who had helped make the revolution of 1917 happen – were shot.

### *To control local Communist Party bosses*

Leaders in Moscow struggled to get local party bosses to do as they were told. Many were friendly with local NKVD commanders, and covered up their own mistakes, while punishing others. There was much corruption. Some local bosses were arrested and shot in order to persuade others to obey orders.

### *To protect the government if a war broke out*

Hitler came to power in 1933; and by 1936, it had become clear that the British and French were not going to punish him for breaking treaties. From the point of view of the Soviet Union, it became increasingly likely that there might soon be a war with Nazi Germany. In which case, anyone threatening Stalin's position at home needed to be dealt with.

### *To blame others for the assassination of Kirov in December 1934*

Kirov was the party boss in Leningrad. He opposed the shooting of Ryutin; and in the Central Committee elections at the 1934 Party Congress he may have gained more votes than Stalin. Kirov resisted attempts by Stalin to move him from Leningrad to Moscow. After Kirov was killed in December 1934, Zinoviev and Kamenev were arrested and accused of involvement in the plot to kill him. But many historians think Stalin was really behind the murder, and used it to destroy his rivals.

### *The weakness of the communist government*

Strong, well-run, popular governments, do not need to terrorise their own people. The mass purges of the Great Terror reveal a government trying to rush the transformation of a vast country it could not fully control. Its reaction, when facing opposition or problems, was to use violence. This was the tried and trusted strategy of a ruthless party that had seized power with violence – and used violence to deal with problems. Added to this, was Stalin's brutal and suspicious personality. But this in itself would not have been enough to launch the Great Terror. Stalin was supported by key people who thought that this really was the way to solve the problems of the Soviet Union. Many of them would later become victims of the terror they had helped to start.

The gunman, Nikolayev, had twice been arrested near Kirov's office. The second time he was carrying a gun. Both times he was released.

Secret police officers responsible for investigating the murder were arrested and later shot.

Kirov's bodyguard was not with him when he was killed. The bodyguard later died in a traffic 'accident'.

Nikolayev was executed without standing trial.

**Figure 3.4** Suspicious circumstances, suggesting Kirov's murder was planned.

## Source A

From Operational Order 00447, 30 July 1937, listing all those who are yet to be destroyed by the NKVD.

Former Kulaks who have escaped from camps, exile, and labour settlements.

Many church officials.

Anti-Soviet political parties (SRs, Mensheviks).

Active members of bandit uprisings.

Whites.

Some of the above mentioned, leaving the countryside for the cities, have infiltrated enterprises of industry, transport and construction. Criminals are still entrenched in both countryside and city. These include horse and cattle thieves, robbers, and others who have been serving their sentences and who have escaped and are now in hiding. The organs of state security [the NKVD] are faced with the task of mercilessly crushing this entire gang of anti-Soviet elements.

## Source B

From a letter written by an ordinary citizen, in August 1936, to Yezhov, head of the NKVD.

On reading in the paper the charges against the fascist hirelings Trotsky, Zinoviev and Co, I could not react calmly — I just do not know how to express my outrage — I felt such hatred towards these scoundrels that I fell to thinking about how all honest Party and non-Party Bolsheviks should keep an eye on their friends and acquaintances: how they breathe, how they live and what they do, in order completely to unmask all traces of Zinovievism — and there are plenty, I suspect.

I want to describe one case: I find it incomprehensible and if anyone needs to know about it, let them look into it...

## Interpretation 3

From *The Great Terror: A Reassessment*, by R. Conquest, published in 1990.

*The simplest form of true answer [to the question 'Why did the terror of the 1930s happen?'] would, of course, be "to destroy or disorientate all possible sources of opposition to Stalin's progress to absolute rule". A vast number of past or potential "hostile" elements had been destroyed or sent to labour camps, and the rest of the population reduced to the most complete silence and obedience.*

## Exam-style question, Section B

Study Interpretations 1 and 2.

How far do you agree with Interpretation 2 about the similarity between Lenin and Stalin's use of terror?

Explain your answer, using both interpretations and your knowledge of the historical context.    **20 marks**

## Exam tip

- Identify how similar the writer of Interpretation 2 thinks Lenin and Stalin were. Note things that were *similar*, and things that were *different*.
- Explain whether, in this historian's opinion, the *similarities* or the *differences* were greater.
- Then decide if you agree with this view, bearing in mind the suggestions from Interpretation 1, and your own weighing up of the evidence.

## Main events of the purges

### A faltering start

After the murder of Kirov, many arrests were made. Those arrested refused to implicate Zinoviev and Kamenev – but were shot anyway. The arrests of people accused of involvement in the murder stopped, but flared up again in 1936.

The head of the NKVD – Yagoda – was arrested, and later shot for being slow to track down enemies of the Soviet Union. His replacement – Yezhov – was told by Stalin that the NKVD was four years behind in unmasking 'enemies'.

## THINKING HISTORICALLY — Evidence (2b&c)

### Evidence and overall judgements

Why did the Great Terror happen? Study Sources A and B and Interpretation 3 .

1  Which of the texts were written on the basis of personal experience of the events?

2  Which of the authors must have based their account on studying evidence rather than on personal experience?

3  Of Sources A and B, which is most useful in helping us assess why Stalin launched the Great Terror in the 1930s?

4  When thinking about the question of overall success, does the historian have an advantage over an eye witness? Explain your answer.

5  If there is evidence that people at the time thought there really were 'enemies of the people' threatening the Soviet Union, why do you think the historian believes the Great Terror was actually set up by Stalin for his own advantage?

6  Is there information in Interpretation 3 that people in 1937–38 probably didn't know? Explain your answer.

7  How do you think the author of Interpretation 3 got his information?

### Attacking the Communist Party and 'wreckers'

Arrests first targeted local Communist Party bosses and party members who were accused of opposing government orders. This accompanied the first 'show trials' in Moscow. Arrests of factory managers who were accused of 'wrecking' (deliberately damaging the Soviet Union) followed. This soon expanded to drag in ordinary people too.

### Mass arrests

The secret police (the NKVD) were given targets of how many 'enemies' they should 'discover'. This led to large numbers being arrested. As people were interrogated (usually for imaginary crimes or just accidents) they confessed and named others involved in their 'crimes'. These too were arrested, confessed, and named others. Things were starting to spiral out of control.

### The 'Time of Yezhov'

In the Soviet Union the worst time of mass arrests and shootings was in 1937–38 – which became known as the 'Yezhovschina' (Time of Yezhov). Yezhov was head of the NKVD, until he, himself, was finally arrested in November 1938 – and later shot. The fact that this period was named after Yezhov reveals a Russian tradition of blaming the person who carried out government policy – rather than the leader who was truly responsible: in this case Stalin.

There was also a strong sense that what people in power did was not the concern of ordinary people. When a group of factory workers was asked what they thought about a show trial of Trostkyites in the 1930s, they replied, 'We clean the floor; *that* doesn't concern us.'

## Source C

From the autobiography of Lev Kopelev, published in 1977, which looks back at his experiences during the Great Terror.

```
I believed that, on balance, Stalin was
right in deciding on these terrible measures
in order to discredit all forms of political
opposition for once and for all. We were a
besieged fortress; we had to be united.
```

## Source D

From a letter sent by Meyerhold, a prisoner at the Butyrki Prison in Moscow, to Molotov, a senior member of the communist government in January 1940.

```
The investigator kept threatening me, 'If
you don't write something (meaning – make
it up!?), we'll beat you again. Only your
head and right hand will be left alone, the
rest of your body we'll reduce to shapeless
bloody shreds.' So I signed everything...
I now retract my confessions, as they were
beaten out of me.
```

## Consequences of the purges

### Destruction of the 'Old Bolsheviks'

The independent-minded members of the Communist Party – who had known and argued with Lenin and were confident of their own opinions – were dead, along with perhaps one million other party members! They were replaced by a new generation who owed everything to Stalin. Stalin was now in total control of the party and the country.

### Weakening of the armed forces

In 1937, leading members of the armed forces were arrested and accused of plotting against Stalin and spying for foreign countries – including Nazi Germany. The armed forces were the only group in the Soviet Union who had the power to threaten Stalin's rule. With the party leadership crushed by earlier arrests and executions, Stalin then turned on this group in order to be totally secure.

There is no evidence that anyone in the military leadership really was threatening Stalin. In fact, Tukhachevsky, the Chief of Staff, was an enthusiastic supporter of Stalin, and supported collectivisation as it promised secure food supplies for the Red Army. The Red Army had expanded and become better equipped because of the Five-Year Plans, and this had increased its power and importance in the Soviet Union. Unfortunately, this had also made Stalin more fearful of it. About 35,000 officers were arrested in 1937 and 1938. Confessions were beaten out of those arrested, before they were tried in 'closed' trials (with no members of the public present).

Once the arrests started, many officers were denounced by their own men. Some of this may have been because of personal disagreements, or a desire to appear loyal to the government and avoid arrest. Many of the most experienced officers were shot, including: three marshals of the Soviet Union*, including Tukhachevsky, the Chief of Staff; half its generals; eight admirals; and 15,000 other officers. Of six senior commanders photographed at a May Day parade in Moscow in 1935 (see Source I) only one survived. This weakened the Soviet Union's defences when Germany invaded in 1941.

### Key term

**Marshals of the Soviet Union***
Highest-ranking military commanders. There were five in 1935 – and three of them were shot.

## Chaos in the economy and government

Experienced members of the government, factory managers, and skilled scientists had been swept away, along with huge numbers of others. The loss of their skills and experience would hold back the further development of the Soviet Union. Also, in a culture of fear, people said what was expected, and were too afraid to ask difficult questions or point out problems. This also caused massive problems in the later development of the country.

## Huge loss of life

Historians still argue fiercely about how many died in the purges – or Great Terror – of the 1930s. Probably about seven to eight million people were arrested in 1937–38: one million of these were shot, and two million died in camps. In 1939, about seven million people were still in labour camps. Many of these died, but it is hard to be sure about exact figures. They must be added to the huge numbers (perhaps seven million) who had died during collectivisation earlier in the 1930s. Altogether the numbers were colossal – and the vast majority were innocent of any crime.

## The labour camp system in the Soviet Union

The term 'the Gulag' is sometimes used to describe the system of labour camps that sprang up across the Soviet Union. In Russian, 'GULAG' stands for 'Main Administration of Corrective Labour Camps'. By 1941, there were about eight million prisoners in labour camps. There may have been as many as a million more in prisons.

Among the different kinds of prisoners could be found:

- peasants arrested during collectivisation
- workers who had been convicted of wrecking
- Communist Party and government officials suspected of sabotage
- foreign communists who had gone to live in the Soviet Union
- artists, writers and university lecturers
- leaders of minority ethnic groups (e.g. Mongols, Kazakhs, Uzbeks)
- members of ethnic minority groups with links to bordering countries (e.g. Poles, Koreans, Chinese)
- huge numbers of people who had simply been arrested to fulfil NKVD arrest quotas.

Slave labourers in the Gulag system were sometimes referred to as 'white coal', because they provided the energy that ran the mines, logging camps and factories in the camps. This vast army felled trees, built roads and railway lines, and mined coal and gold.

These prisoners – called '*zeks*' within the camp system – were used to open up undeveloped areas of the north and east of the Soviet Union and Siberia. In the far east, the labour camps of the Eastern Construction Trust, in the Kolyma river valley, occupied an area as large as France. In the arctic regions, hundreds of 'Camps of Complete Isolation' were located in some of the wildest and most inhospitable areas of the Soviet Union.

Prisoners working in the camps faced long, hard hours, on little food. Working in thin uniforms, and sleeping in scarcely heated huts, they faced sub-zero temperatures in the winter, and terrible working conditions and punishments. Over one winter in the Kolyma region, camps cut off by the snow were later found to have lost every one of their inhabitants, including the guards and their dogs. It was a savage world, where vast numbers died.

**Figure 3.5** The labour camp system in the Soviet Union in the 1930s: the 'Gulag'.

## Source E

From the Russian novel *Doctor Zhivago*, written by Boris Pasternak and published in 1957. Here the narrator describes the fate of one of the main characters, Laura.

```
One day [she] went out and did not come back.
She must have been arrested in the street
at that time. She vanished without a trace
and probably died somewhere, forgotten as a
nameless number on a list that afterwards
got mislaid, in one of the innumerable mixed
or women's concentration camps in the north.
```

## Show trials, 1936–38

The leading Communist Party members were tried and found guilty of fictional crimes at 'show trials'. These were designed to put on trial the most famous prisoners. Ordinary people either had no trial at all or, at most, a quick appearance before a three-man NKVD *troika*. So the show trials were part of the purges, but only affected a relatively small number of people.

## Source F

Official Soviet photograph from 1932, showing labour camp prisoners working on the White Sea-Baltic Canal.

## Activity ?

Based on what you have learned in this chapter, how accurate is the depiction of the impact of mass arrests in Source F? Write a speech, to present to the class, on what you think it was like to live in the Soviet Union in this period of time.

Show trials were 'political theatre': the charges were fictional, the speeches pre-scripted, the outcome pre-determined. The idea was to convince people across the Soviet Union that those on trial really were traitors. These show trials were part of the intensification of purging that happened in 1936–38. They took place in Moscow, and films of them were released to the world's press. Zinoviev and Kamenev were put on trial in 1936. They 'confessed' to taking part in terrorism organised by the exiled Trotsky. They were found guilty and shot. In 1937, Trotsky's ally, Piatakov, was tried and shot for plotting against Stalin. In 1938, Bukharin was tried and shot. He had pleaded guilty – as had the others.

## Extend your knowledge

### The deaths of Stalin's old rivals

After his trial, Bukharin wrote a letter to Stalin. It contained the question: 'Koba [a nickname for Stalin], why do you need me to die?' When Stalin later died, in 1953, the note was found in his private desk. He had kept it for more than a decade. Nobody knows why. Perhaps it reminded him of how he had triumphed over those who had once looked down on him.

Similarly, during late-night drinking sessions, Stalin's bodyguard would amuse him by retelling how Zinoviev had begged on his knees for mercy before being shot. The secret police kept two bullets neatly labelled 'Zinoviev' and 'Kamenev' – the ones used to kill them.

The show trials were used to destroy old opponents of Stalin, and justify the mass arrests, by getting people to confess to lists of imaginary crimes. Why did they confess? Probably for a mixture of reasons: to try and protect their families; in the hope of having mercy shown (it was not); because they still believed in the Communist Party, and still wished to serve it; and some may have been tortured into confessing.

### *The importance of the show trials*

The confessions of those tried in the show trials persuaded many people within the Soviet Union, and some communists abroad, that there really was a threat to the Soviet Union from these 'enemies of the people'. They also gave the government somebody to blame for the problems facing the Soviet Union. During the Time

of Yezhov, they were a way by which the government tried to convince ordinary people that mass arrests really were necessary.

In addition, the show trials encouraged ordinary workers to denounce their managers for things that frustrated them – without the blame going as far as Stalin and the highest leadership of the Soviet Union. In this way – even as the purges were destroying millions of people – there is evidence for popular support for them from many workers, who were keen to denounce both hated factory managers and local Communist Party officials. These workers felt that the government was finally allowing them to have an influence on how the Soviet Union was run.

## Source G

A newspaper photograph showing leading communists (including Bukharin) approving death sentence verdicts at the 'Trial of the Twenty-one' in 1938.

## Source H

The senior commanders of the Red Army salute a parade on May Day, 1935.

## Activities **?**

1 Why did the communist government release photographs like Source H to the world?

2 Does this suggest that those tried at the show trials were guilty? Explain your answer.

3 Why were the show trials important to Stalin; and what part did they play in the Great Terror of the 1930s?

## Summary

- The purges, or Great Terror, of the 1930s occurred for a number of reasons – not just because Stalin wanted to destroy all opposition to his rule.
- What started as the removal of local party bosses and factory managers, soon accelerated into mass arrests that swept up millions of people.
- Huge numbers of innocent people were killed, or imprisoned in the Gulag camp system.
- In 1936–38, the show trials targeted the most high-profile of those who had been arrested.

## Checkpoint

### Strengthen

**S1** What was the NKVD? What part did it play in the use of terror in the 1930s?

**S2** What evidence is there that Stalin may have been behind the murder of Kirov?

**S3** What was the Gulag? What part did it play in the use of terror in the 1930s?

### Challenge

**C1** 'The murder of Kirov was the event that led to the mass arrests of the 1930s'. To what extent do you agree with this commonly held opinion?

**C2** Based on the evidence, which of these ways of understanding why the mass arrests occurred do you find most convincing?

   **a** A brutal plan by Stalin to increase his power.

   **b** A chaotic response by the government to problems in a country it found hard to control.

How confident do you feel about your answers? Compare your answers with that of a neighbour. Review each other's ideas, giving feedback on what is well argued and what could be explained more clearly.

## Learning outcomes

- Know about government control of art and the media.
- Know about government control of religion and education.
- Understand why Stalin introduced a new Soviet Constitution in 1936.

## The link between 'terror' and the control of information

There is evidence that ordinary people tended to assume that when *other people* were arrested, it was because they were guilty, but if *they themselves* were arrested, then there must have been a mistake. It was not just fear that kept people in line and obedient to the government of Stalin; they still believed in the communist system – even in the midst of upheaval and mass arrests. This belief was encouraged by the government's control over information, and by the 'official culture', which supported the aims of the government and the Communist Party.

## 'Official culture' in the Soviet Union

The government of the Soviet Union was keen to control the hearts and minds of the people – shaping their ideas, and their views of the country and the world. In order to do this, it kept a firm grasp on the information and ideas made available to the people. The aim was for all expressions of ideas, and all available information, to be brought into line with the outlook of Stalin and the Communist Party.

A system in which a dictator has total control over the lives of the citizens of the country, and the information they can access, is known as a 'totalitarian dictatorship'. Few governments can achieve this. Today we know that Stalin was not able to bring every source of ideas completely under his control. The Soviet Union was just too large and complicated – with different groups competing for influence and holding conflicting and alternative views.

These groups included: the Communist Party; the NKVD secret police; the army; officials running the economy and setting targets; peasants who ran away from collective farms; workers who tried to get factories run in ways that benefitted them; members of the middle class from tsarist times, who tried to reinvent themselves in order to survive; and members of minority ethnic and religious groups. Nobody could assert their views openly, but there were conflicts and competition, and not everything fell in line with Stalin's will. This is one of the reasons why the murderous purges occurred.

Nevertheless, Stalin got a long way in his attempt to bring the Soviet Union under his total control – and the creation of 'official culture' was part of this. Culture was to be one of the weapons used to control people and make them obedient to the will of Stalin and his government. All expressions of ideas – from lessons in schools to posters on factory noticeboards – were to be in keeping with the aims of the government.

### Socialist realism

This attempt to control culture – so that it served the needs of the communist dictatorship under Stalin – can be seen clearly in the world of art. In the 1920s, a style and philosophy known as 'socialist realism' emerged. By the 1930s, it was the most influential style of art in the Soviet Union. Outstanding socialist realist artists of the period included: Kuzma Petrov-Vodkin, Isaak Brodsky, Alexander Samokhvalov, Alexander Deineka and Yuri Pimenov.

In 1932, Stalin published a decree: 'On the Reconstruction of Literary and Art Organisation'. This put socialist realism at the centre of Stalin's attempt to control culture. Shortly afterwards, the Moscow and Leningrad Union of Artists was established, to ensure all art was in line with the new rules.

Socialist realism had to be simple, easy to understand, and carry a clear message. It was to show people in ordinary situations – at work, in factories and steelworks, and on farms – but present these situations as vital to modernising and developing the Soviet Union. Workers should look like heroes, and their work should look important. The same ideas were also to apply to novels and to music. All were to be made to follow the rules of socialist realism.

Stalin described those who produced socialist realism as being 'engineers of souls'. By this, he meant that they would create a new kind of person, who felt differently about themselves and the world. These 'new people' would be enthusiastic about building a communist Soviet Union, and would believe in its values and goals.

## Source A

An official state painting: 'Before starting their shift', by Alexei Alexandrovich, painted in 1937.

## Source B

'For Collectivisation! For the Harvest!', painted in 1940. This image was created for an official poster, by Vasily Kostyanitsyn, in 1940. The banners read, "To the elections! For collectivisation! For the harvest!"

## Source C

An official poster, issued in 1939. The text says, 'Woman, get on the locomotive!'

## Activities ?

1 Look carefully at Sources A, B, and C. For each one, say how it is an example of socialist realism. Identify its 'message' and how the image communicates this message.

2 Write a 50-word paragraph explaining what socialist realism was. Read it to a neighbour, and get them to decide how well you have summed it up, and any ways you could improve it.

3 Why was 'official culture' important in building a communist dictatorship in the Soviet Union?

## Government control of education
### The Cultural Revolution

Through reform of the educational curriculum, and increased control of education, Stalin tightened his grip on the next generation of Soviet citizens. In the early 1930s, there was a great upheaval in education known as the 'Cultural Revolution'. It took place at the same time as the first Five-Year Plans and collectivisation were introduced, see Chapter 4. It was part of Stalin's attempt to drive the Soviet Union forward, and get rid of old ways of life and old ways of doing things.

School students were encouraged to denounce their teachers if they appeared to lack enthusiasm for communism. There was an end to school discipline, uniforms and exams. Workers were given more encouragement in education than people from middle-class backgrounds. Middle-class young people were often thrown out of school. While this allowed a new generation of workers to get an education – it also caused chaos.

### Restoring order

By the mid-1930s, the 'Cultural Revolution' had achieved what Stalin wanted: old-fashioned teachers and middle-class students had been driven out, and a new generation of educated workers produced – who owed everything to the Communist Party. It was now time to bring discipline and order back to education. School uniforms were reintroduced, and girls were even expected to wear their hair braided in traditional pig-tails. Once again, fees were charged for top senior school and higher education.

At the same time, new textbooks were produced. People who had been purged were written out of history as if they had never existed. History was rewritten to make it seem that Stalin had been Lenin's right-hand man. There was a core curriculum in maths, science, a foreign language, history and geography, that every student had to follow – which was designed to convey Stalin's view of life and the world.

## Government attacks on religion
### Orthodox Christianity

Communists were atheists, and opposed to all forms of religion. So the Orthodox Church had faced pressure from the communists since 1917, especially as it had supported the tsar and the Whites in the Civil War. Now, it was attacked, and many churches were shut down. Priests were shot or imprisoned, and persecution increased, as Stalin tried to wipe out religion in the Soviet Union.

Colleges for training priests were closed, and religious publications and religious education for children were banned. By 1941, only 500 churches remained open: there had been 54,000 in 1914. The churches that were closed down included very ancient churches such as: the Alexander Nevsky Cathedral in Baku, demolished in 1937; Kazan Cathedral in Moscow, demolished in 1936 to give tanks access to Red Square for military parades; and the Cathedral of Christ the Saviour, also in Moscow, demolished in 1931 to make way for a building to house the Supreme Soviet of the Soviet Union. The latter was never built and, instead, the world's largest open air swimming pool was later located on the site.

However, despite the persecution, the communists were not able to destroy the Orthodox Church, because too many citizens of the Soviet Union remained members.

### Islam

Muslims too found themselves under attack. This especially impacted on Sufi* groups in the southern republics. However, anyone who stood out as not fitting into the new Soviet system was in danger. Many Muslims were treated as dangerous because they had loyalty towards a religion that existed outside of the Soviet Union. They were put under pressure to stop using the Arabic script in their writing, as it was felt to link them to foreigners. Many non-Russian speakers were also made to speak Russian. Local leaders were shot, as they were accused of being nationalists who wanted independence from the Soviet Union. Mosques, Muslim schools and Islamic courts were shut. Campaigns against women wearing the veil took place in Uzbekistan. Going on Hajj to Mecca was banned. Other Muslim communities suffered as nomadic tribes were forced to join collective farms in Kazakhstan.

| Key term |
| --- |
| **Sufi***
Muslims following a mystical form of Islam, which seeks a direct personal experience of God. |

## *Judaism*

Jews living in the Soviet Union also faced increasing pressure during the 1930s. Anti-semitism was illegal – but many religious Jews still faced discrimination. Due to official opposition towards Jews who wanted to emigrate to the Middle East, Stalin set up an area in the far east of the Soviet Union called the Jewish Autonomous Oblast (district). The hope was that Jews would choose to go and live there. It was not a success; and local Jewish leaders in the Jewish Autonomous Oblast fell victim to the purges, just as people did across the Soviet Union.

## *Buddhism*

Buddhists in the Soviet Union also suffered. Buddhist teachers were expelled or arrested as 'Japanese spies'. Among the Kalmyk people of southern Russia, Buddhist monasteries were shut, Buddhist monks and Buddhist livestock herders were sent to Siberia, and religious texts were destroyed.

## Media censorship

Everything that was read (including newspapers, novels and poetry), viewed or heard, had to be positive about Stalin and the Communist Party. The Communist Party and Stalin were being presented as alternatives to any other kind of beliefs or faith. All problems in the Soviet Union were blamed on deliberate wrecking by 'enemies of the people'. This was designed to make people accept that the purges really were necessary, and that any problems were not the government's fault.

Media censorship was extensive. The writings of people who had been purged were made to disappear from the Soviet Union. For example, all of Trotsky's work was banned, and anyone caught owning one of his publications was arrested as a 'Trotskyist oppositionist'. Trotsky was literally airbrushed out of photographs, along with other people who had been purged. It was all designed to make it seem as if they had never existed. In addition, a government body called Glavlit (short for Main Administration for Literary and Publishing Affairs) controlled all publication of economic data. This meant that there was no independent way of checking whether government claims about the economy were really true. Only the views of the government could be read in the Soviet Union.

## Source D

Two photographs of Lenin giving a speech. In the second, the government censor has removed Trotsky, who can be seen standing to the right of the platform in the photograph on the left.

There were a number of consequences of media censorship:

- Without any other sources of information, many people simply believed what they read and saw. The alternative was to believe that nothing could be trusted – and that was hard to accept.
- Many people had only a limited education – and did not have the confidence to question the 'official truth'.
- On the other hand, not everyone believed what they were told – and rumours, whispers and half-truths spread among those who were not convinced.
- The Soviet Union became a country in which it was difficult to check or verify anything – and where it was safest to just accept what you were told.

In the short term, this increased Stalin's power; but, in the long term, it was very bad for the development of the Soviet Union. A country in which farmers dared not talk about crop diseases, factory managers could not discuss problems in the supply of raw materials, and the military could not criticise poor equipment, was heading for trouble.

# The new Soviet Constitution of 1936

In 1936 – just as the terrible wave of mass arrests was starting – Stalin's government brought out a new constitution*.

| Key term ▶ |
| --- |
| **Constitution***<br>A document detailing how a country is governed and the rights of its citizens. |

The constitution promised key rights – but few of these rights actually existed in the communist dictatorship. This raises the question of why Stalin did this, at a time when people's basic rights and freedom were actually being crushed, and millions of lives were about to be destroyed. There are a number of possible answers:

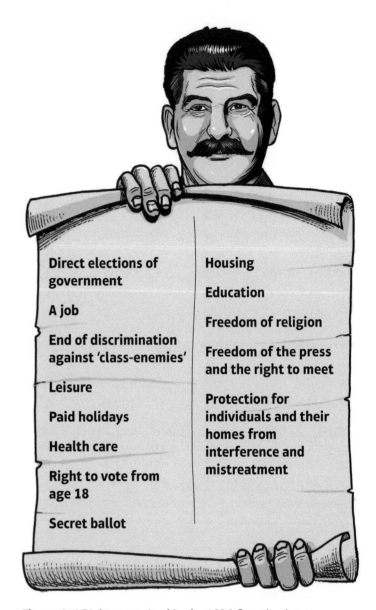

**Figure 3.6** Rights promised in the 1936 Constitution.

- It sent a message that the Soviet Union had been transformed since the time of the 1924 Constitution – and aimed to increase support among ordinary people.
- Introducing a secret ballot and giving young people the right to vote made the Soviet Union *seem* democratic – as a way of inspiring support from its citizens. Encouraging people to discuss the constitution, and contribute ideas, made them believe that they were really involved in decision-making.

- It helped persuade people whose parents had been middle class, or kulaks, to support the Soviet Union – since it claimed they were no longer facing discrimination because of their class origins.

- It made the system of Soviet government look attractive to people abroad. This was important as Stalin feared the rise of Nazi Germany, and he wanted democratic countries in the West to feel more positive about the Soviet Union and be willing to work with it.

Stalin was attempting to appeal to ordinary Soviet citizens, at the same time as he was sweeping away local factory managers and local Communist Party bosses. It made him look like a leader who cared about the *ordinary* people. Like socialist realism, the new constitution encouraged people to 'buy into' the official idea of what the Soviet Union was like – despite the hardship, chaos and brutality that was actually happening in everyday life.

It promoted the idea that there were 'winners' as well as 'losers' in the Soviet Union. The 'losers' were those who deserved punishment for spoiling the country by their 'crimes' – but for those who were not purged, the Soviet Union really was getting better.

## Interpretation 1

From *Origins of the Great Purges: The Soviet Communist Party Reconsidered, 1933–1938*, by J. Arch Getty, published in 1987.

*1937 would see radicals [in the Communist Party] try to realise and even extend the provisions [terms] of the Stalin Constitution and use it as a weapon against the bureaucracy [government officials]. As the wave of popular radicalism [widespread political involvement] mounted in early 1937, such attempts helped to provoke a political crisis.*

## Interpretation 2

From *Stalinist Values: The Cultural Norms of Soviet Modernity,1917–1941*, by D. Lloyd Hoffmann, published in 2003.

*Stalin used the Constitution to enhance the legitimacy of the Soviet system in the eyes of both domestic [Soviet] and foreign observers. Defining the structures of the state constitutionally added to its respectability and helped to centralise its power. In this sense the Constitution was part of Stalin's broader effort to... create reliable central [government] agencies to carry out his orders. The Constitution, while it did not in fact place any limits on the Party leader's authoritarian rule, also made the Soviet Union appear more democratic.*

## Exam-style question, Section B

Study Interpretations 1 and 2. They give different views about the effects of the 1936 Constitution.

What is the main difference between these views?

Explain your answer, using details from both interpretations.

**4 marks**

## Exam tip

Firstly, sum up the views of each interpretation. Then identify the main difference. Support your answer using both interpretations.

## Summary

- Under Stalin's rule there was a determined effort by the government to control all media.
- The aim of this was to ensure that people only had access to communist ideas.
- There was also an attempt to control ideas in education and suppress religion.
- The 1936 Constitution was designed to persuade people that the Soviet Union was being transformed for the better under communist rule and the leadership of Stalin.

## Checkpoint

### Strengthen

**S1** For each of the following, write two sentences, one saying why Stalin wanted to control it, and one saying how he tried to do it: art, education, religion, access to information.

**S2** What is a 'constitution'? Explain what the 1936 one promised.

**S3** What is 'censorship'? Describe ways it was used in the Soviet Union in the 1930s.

### Challenge

**C1** How did Stalin use art and education as a way of increasing his power as dictator?

**C2** Why do you think that Stalin brought in a new constitution in 1936 – promising all kinds of freedoms – just as he was actually destroying freedom in the Soviet Union and killing millions of people?

How confident do you feel about your answers to these questions? Review them with a partner, then help each other to write new, improved answers.

# 3.4 The cult of Stalin

## Learning outcomes

- Understand why the 'cult of Stalin' was created.
- Be able to describe how Stalin was presented in official communications.

## The cult of the wise and kind leader in Russia... and the blame game

Russia had a tradition of separating leaders from unpopular decisions. In tsarist times, the tsar was often referred to as 'the little father' – and unpopular aspects of life were blamed on somebody else.

The communists took over this method. First Lenin, and then Stalin, were presented as wise and just leaders, who cared for ordinary people, were simple in their tastes (this was actually true), and had the wisdom to lead and unite the newly-formed Soviet Union. This focus on an individual is sometimes called the 'cult of personality'. Because the Soviet Union – despite the communist revolution – still had an ancient religious tradition, this often had a very religious feel about it. While they would have denied it, the way that Lenin and Stalin were treated almost formed part of a godless religion. In place of a religious faith was the Communist Party, with its promises of a better life. In place of priests and prophets were the leaders of the party.

When there were problems, those blamed were 'class enemies'. These included: surviving middle-class people pretending to be workers in the new Soviet Union; peasant kulaks in the countryside; and opposition politicians, such as the old Mensheviks, anarchists and communists, who had lost out in the power struggle of the 1920s. Lenin was arrogant, and could be brutal, but he was not personally insecure or desperate to be praised. Stalin was different: he seems to have been personally insecure, bore grudges for years, and demanded unquestioning praise and support. Once he was in power, the 'cult of Stalin' began to develop. With the problems of the 1930s, the cult became even more important.

## Creating the cult of Stalin

There were two important political reasons why the 'cult of Stalin' was created in the Soviet Union in the 1930s.

1  It put Stalin beyond criticism. In a country facing many problems and upheavals, this focus on one man offered a sense of stability. It gave the impression that however chaotic things were, there was one man who could make sense of it all.

2  It presented Stalin as 'the new Lenin' who could be the centre point of loyalty. Once Lenin had died, a 'cult of Lenin' had developed, and somebody else was needed to continue it. That person was Stalin. This strengthened his ruling position – as he was presented as the 'Leader, Teacher and Friend' of all the people of the Soviet Union.

The 'cult of Stalin' also existed to increase support for the communist regime. It offered a way of working round problems without needing to question one-party rule: local party members might make a mess of things, but the leader of the party could fix everything.

## Extend your knowledge

### Confidence in Stalin

The writer Erenburg later recalled how, in 1937, at the height of the mass arrests and the cult of Stalin, he met another writer, Boris Pasternak, while out walking one night in Moscow. Pasternak cried out: 'If only someone would tell Stalin about all this!' Propaganda had worked so well that he clearly assumed the 'kind and fair' Stalin knew nothing about the mass arrests and suffering going on in the Soviet Union.

## The 'official' Stalin

**Stalin was presented as a political 'genius':** he was presented as the one person who fully understood the communist way and could explain life and point the way into the future. However, Stalin was careful not to make this claim himself – and never used the word 'Stalinism' to describe his ideas. Instead, he presented himself as the person who understood Lenin's ideas ('Leninism' or 'Marxist-Leninism') better than anyone else. This made him seem humble – while putting him above criticism.

**Stalin was praised for economic 'advances':** posters associated Stalin with the latest achievements of the Soviet Union. He was pictured against a background of factories, trains and happy collective farmers bringing in the harvest using tractors. It was as if every technological and economic improvement was due to his actions. In fact, he rarely even visited factories or farms.

**Stalin was presented as fatherly, kind and loved by all:** posters pictured Stalin surrounded by children, applauded by workers, and gazed at adoringly, as if he was an all-knowing and loving father-figure. But, once again – apart from some carefully stage-managed events – Stalin rarely mixed with ordinary people outside his close circle within the government.

### Source A

From *Journey Into the Whirlwind*, an autobiographical account of life in the Gulag, by E. Ginzburg, published in 1967.

At the camp, I was to come across many people who managed strangely to combine a sane judgement of what was going on in the country with a truly mystical personal cult of Stalin.

### Interpretation 1

From *A People's Tragedy*, by O. Figes, published in 1996. He is describing the relationship between Stalin and a leading Russian writer, named Gorky.

*After Gorky's death a large oil-skin notebook was found in his belongings in which he compared Stalin to a 'monstrous flea' which 'propaganda and the hypnosis of fear have enlarged to incredible proportions'. There is evidence to suggest that by 1934 Gorky had become involved in a plot against Stalin... Gorky's involvement with the opposition makes it just as likely that Stalin murdered him... Many years later it was claimed that the doctors involved in Gorky's autopsy had found traces of poison in the corpse.*

The messages that built the cult of Stalin were communicated through graphic design, art, literature, music and history books.

## Graphic art

Posters were put up in factories, at collective farms and on the streets. Specially commissioned paintings and prints claimed to show the kind of leader Stalin was, and his relationship with the people. Because these were artworks – they did not have to be based on reality. They often showed Stalin as a close friend of Lenin – which he was not – or planning the October Revolution – which was actually masterminded by Trotsky.

## Written and spoken word

Books, poems, songs and plays were written, dedicated to Stalin and praising him. Some of the poetry spoke of him as if he was superhuman – some even used religious terms.

Two histories of the Communist Party, published in 1938, hailed Stalin's role as 'the Lenin of today'. These books rewrote history and placed Stalin in the centre of events. Stalin's role in the October Revolution and winning the Civil War was exaggerated, and Trotsky – who had actually played a much more important role – was totally ignored.

## Source B

A painting from 1938 of Lenin and Stalin by the state-approved artist Nikolay Shestopalov.

## Activities ?

1  How did Russian history help prepare people for the communist cults of Lenin and Stalin?

2  Create a spidergram describing the 'cult of Stalin'. Include information on: what it was, why it was introduced, how it was spread, and what it achieved.

3  Look carefully at Sources B, and C. What impression does each try to give you of Stalin? How does it try to do this? Why was this useful for Stalin's rule?

## Source C

An official poster, issued in 1936. The text says, 'Thank you, dear Stalin, for a happy childhood!'

## Source D

From a speech made by the writer Avdienko, in praise of Stalin, at the 1935 Congress of Soviets.

The men of all ages will call upon thy name, which is strong, beautiful, wise and marvellous. Thy name is engraven [carved] on every factory, every machine, every place on the earth, and in the hearts of all men.

I write books. I am an author. All thanks to thee, O great educator, Stalin. I love a young woman with a renewed love and shall perpetuate [continue] myself in my children — all thanks to thee, great educator, Stalin. I shall be eternally happy and joyous, all thanks to thee, great educator, Stalin. Everything belongs to thee, chief of our great country. And when the woman I love presents me with a child the first word it shall utter will be: Stalin.

## Source E

A poem that appeared in the official communist newspaper, *Pravda*, in August 1936.

```
O great Stalin, O leader of the peoples,
Thou who broughtest man to birth.
Thou who fructifiest [makes fruitful] the earth,
Thou who restorest the centuries,
Thou who makest bloom the spring,
Thou who makest vibrate the musical chords...
Thou, splendour of my spring, O Thou,
Sun reflected by millions of hearts...
```

### Activity ?

Imagine you are either attending the congress (Source D) or reading *Pravda* (Source E). Explain what the sources were designed to make you feel about Stalin.

### THINKING HISTORICALLY  Interpretations (2c/3a)

#### History as hypotheses

In science, you might have come across the idea of a **hypothesis** – a hypothesis is an idea that a scientist comes up with to explain what they can see happening. The scientist then tries to find evidence, through experiments, to find out whether their hypothesis is correct. Historians often work in a similar way, but look at sources to find their evidence, rather than doing experiments.

These three historians are thinking about reasons for the cult of Stalin.

| Historian's interests | Historian's hypothesis | Evidence |
|---|---|---|
| Political historian: interested in leaders, their views and actions and the effects these had on history. | | |
| Economic historian: interested in how economic conditions changed, and how this affected politics and society. | | |
| Cultural historian: interested in changes in how people think, what they read and listen to, and their day-to-day lives. | *The main intention of the cult of Stalin was to create a belief system that would replace religion as a way of offering hope and guidance.* | |

1 Working in groups of three, make a copy of the above table.
   a As a group, discuss the interests of each of the historians, and write a hypothesis that they might put forward based on their interests (one has been done for you as an example).
   b Each person in the group should take on the role of one of the historians. For your historian, add at least three pieces of evidence into the table that support your hypothesis, based on the information and sources in this chapter.
   c For your historian, write a concluding paragraph, summing up your views on the reasons for the cult of Stalin. Remember to restate your hypothesis and support it with your evidence.
2 Share your concluding paragraphs with the rest of the group and compare them.
   a Underline instances where different hypotheses use the same or similar evidence.
   b Look at each hypothesis in turn. Can you think of at least one piece of evidence that challenges each hypothesis? (Tip: you can start by looking at evidence for the other hypotheses being right!)
3 As a group, discuss the question: 'Is it possible to say which hypothesis is correct?'

## Summary

- The 'cult of Stalin' was designed to increase support for Stalin.
- It aimed to make him the one unifying feature of life in the Soviet Union.
- It aimed to remove any blame from him for the problems people faced in the 1930s.

## Checkpoint

### Strengthen

**S1** Write a short paragraph explaining what the 'cult of Stalin' was and why it was introduced.

**S2** Write a short paragraph explaining ways in which it was communicated to people.

### Challenge

**C1** Why do you think many Russian people were prepared to believe in the cult of Stalin?

**C2** Explain how it was possible for an intelligent person like Pasternak to say what he did.

How confident do you feel about your answers to these questions? Reread this section, then try answering them again.

# Recap: Stalin's rise to power and dictatorship, 1924–41

## Recall quiz

1  In what document did Lenin criticise Stalin?
2  Which of Stalin's rivals for power was the first to be defeated?
3  Which of Stalin's rivals continued to support the idea of the NEP?
4  Who was the NKVD chief who led the mass arrests in 1937–38?
5  What was the name of the labour camp system in the Soviet Union?
6  What was 'white coal'?
7  What powerful group in the Soviet Union was purged in 1937?
8  What name was given to art which was designed to communicate the communist outlook?
9  In what year did the Soviet Union get a new constitution?
10  What phrase is used to describe the way Stalin was put at the centre of life and achievement?

## Activities

1  Look at the following questions and answer each with a short paragraph. Note: some of the answers will require you to use information from this chapter only, some involve using information from this chapter **and** from earlier in the book.

   a  How did Stalin's use of terror compare with that of Lenin?

   b  Why did Stalin win the power struggle that took place after the death of Lenin?

   c  Explain the different ways in which the communist government used art as a way of communicating its ideas, aims and values under **both** Lenin and Stalin.

2  Historians hold very different opinions on **why** Stalin launched the Great Terror in the 1930s. This is for a number of reasons:

   • Looking at evidence from central government in Moscow can give a very 'top down' view of events. This tends to make one focus on what the government wanted to happen. It gives the impression that things happened if the government ordered it.

   • Looking at evidence from the regions outside Moscow gives more of a 'bottom up' view of events, and includes the role of: factory managers struggling to meet targets; workers frustrated with poor living and working conditions and looking for someone to blame; local party bosses and factory managers working together to try to protect themselves; local NKVD trying to meet arrest targets; and people moving from job to job.

   • Some historians approach the study of decision-making by looking at what leaders wanted and their intentions.

   • Some historians look at wider groups and events that limited what leaders could do and put pressures on them.

Thinking about these things, write a short paragraph explaining why historians disagree; then give your own opinion on which of the points above you think is most important when trying to decide why Stalin launched the Great Terror in the 1930s.

# Writing historically: explaining and evaluating

You need to think about the purpose of your writing to help you structure it and choose how you express your ideas.

## Learning outcomes

By the end of this lesson, you will understand how to:

- use the key features of explanatory and analytical writing
- structure your writing to ensure you explain or evaluate effectively.

## Definitions

**Explain:** to make an idea clear using relevant facts, details and examples.

**Evaluate:** to examine two or more points of view closely, and carefully, in order to make a judgement or come to a conclusion.

What are the similarities and differences in writing to **explain** and writing to **evaluate**?

Compare these two exam-style questions:

**Question A**

> Explain why the tsar's rule ended in 1917. **(12 marks)**

**Question B**

> How far do you agree with Interpretation 2 (page 85) about the similarity between Lenin and Stalin's use of terror?
>
> Explain your answer, using Interpretations 1 (page 85) and 2 and your knowledge of the historical context. **(16 marks)**

1. Look at the statements below. Which apply to Question A, which to Question B, and which to both? This kind of question:
   a. asks you to write to explain.
   b. asks you to evaluate.
   c. asks you to consider arguments for and against a point of view and reach a conclusion.
   d. requires you to explain how and why an event happened or a situation came about.
   e. requires you to provide evidence and examples to support your ideas.
   f. requires you to link all your ideas to key points.
   g. requires you to explain at least one sequence of events and their consequences.
   h. requires you to consider what contributed to a situation or event.
   i. requires you to link and develop your ideas logically to form a line of reasoning.
   j. requires you to demonstrate good knowledge and understanding of the features or characteristics of the historical period.
   k. requires you to explore how and why a series of circumstances, events or actions led to a particular outcome.

2. Look at your answers to Question 1. What are the key differences between questions that ask you to 'explain why' and questions that ask you 'how far do you agree'?

**How can I structure writing to explain and writing to evaluate?**

**3.** Answers to 'explain why' questions often follow this structure: 1st point; 2nd point; 3rd point; summary of causes and effects that led to a specific outcome.

**4.** The starts of some sentences have been written out below in answer to Question A. Put the sentences in the order in which you think they should appear.

> a. Russia experienced huge losses in the fighting of the First World War...
>
> b. A number of factors combined in early 1917 which eventually led to the fall of the tsar.
>
> c. Finally, the tsar's decision to order the military to disperse protesters was significant...
>
> d. Economic problems caused by the war led to shortages and protests...
>
> e. The tsar's decision to take control of the military caused great problems to his rule...

**5.** Now look at the plan below for an answer to exam-style question B, which asks you to evaluate. Remember, in the exam you would need to refer to both interpretations in the question.

| | |
|---|---|
| 1st point to support the interpretation | a. Far fewer people were killed in Lenin's use of terror |
| 2nd point to support the interpretation | b. Lenin allowed greater room for debate within the Communist Party |
| Signal a turning point in the argument | c. However, Interpretation 2 puts too much emphasis on the differences between them... |
| 1st point to contradict the interpretation | d. Some historians would argue that Lenin like Stalin committed terrible cruelty... |
| 2nd point to contradict the interpretation | e. Under both leaders the country was a dictatorship... |
| Conclusion: a judgement directly responding to the interpretation | f. On balance, there are different ways to assess the impact of terror and Interpretation 2 is correct that there were differences in the way that terror was used... |

**6.** Look at these exam-style questions:

> Explain how the structure of government in the USSR allowed the Communist Party to dominate the country. **(12 marks)**
>
> How far do you agree with Interpretation 2 (see page 22) about why the February Revolution of 1917 occurred?
>
> Explain your answer using Interpretations 2 and 1 (see page 22 and page 21) and your knowledge of the historical context. **(16 marks)**

Plan an answer to each one, using the same structures as the responses above. Write the first sentence of each paragraph.

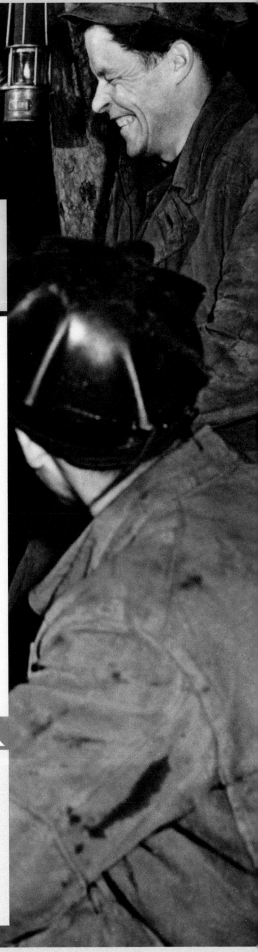

# 04 | Economic and social changes, 1924–41

Stalin, and many others in the Communist Party, were very unhappy with the NEP. They felt it gave too much power to peasants and private traders, and feared this could lead to the revival of capitalism in the Soviet Union. They also felt that it was taking too long to modernise the country.

Their solution was collectivisation – a programme intended to bring agriculture under state control. Grain would be taken from collective farms and sold abroad to raise money to industrialise the Soviet Union. At the same time, Five-Year Plans – setting targets for the rapid growth of industry – were launched.

Collectivisation and the Five-Year Plans had huge impacts on life in the Soviet Union. In the countryside, millions starved, and huge numbers of peasants were arrested for resisting collectivisation. In the new industrial towns, workers lived in poor conditions, and accidents were common, as the country raced to industrialise. Heavy industry became far more productive, but there were few consumer goods and life was hard.

More women were at work than ever before, but they received lower wages than men, and were less likely to get promoted. At the same time, ethnic minorities found life increasingly hard, as they were regarded with suspicion by the state.

In all these areas Stalin was the driving force.

## Learning outcomes

By the end of this chapter you will:

- understand why Stalin collectivised agriculture, and know about the consequences of collectivisation
- know why Stalin launched the Five-Year Plans and about their impact on the Soviet Union
- know what it was like to live and work in the Soviet Union at this time
- understand the impact of communist rule on the lives of women and ethnic minorities.

# 4.1 Agriculture and collectivisation

## Stalin's reasons for changing agriculture

Stalin had many reasons to take control of agriculture* in the Soviet Union.

- Some were **political** – as he wanted more control over the countryside, and finally to defeat Bukharin who was a supporter of the NEP.
- Some were **economic** – as money gained by selling grain aboard could pay for rapid industrialisation and he could attempt to modernise farming.
- Others were **ideological** – as Stalin and many communists feared that peasants were 'little capitalists' and needed to be brought under control. This idea was popular among workers, who felt that peasants were getting more from the revolution than they were.

### Timeline
#### Collectivisation of agriculture

**1927** War scare in the USSR

**1927–28** Grain shortages

**1928** Start of collectivisation

**1929** Start of 'liquidation of the kulaks'

**1930** Temporary halt to collectivisation

**1933** End of collectivisation campaign; collectivisation famine

## Communist ideology and attitudes to agriculture

Stalin – like Lenin before him, and the whole of the Communist Party – was a Marxist (see Section 1.1). Marxists believed that the ideas of Karl Marx (who lived in the 19th century) accurately explained how history progressed over time; how and why people co-operated and clashed with each other; and how this would continue into the future. According to Marxist beliefs:

- the highest stage of human development occurred when countries industrialised and factories produced large quantities of goods
- a traditional rural society, in which most people lived in the countryside and worked in agriculture, would be replaced by an urban society, in which most people lived in towns and cities and worked in factories
- private property would be replaced by shared ownership; and wealth would be redistributed so there was no longer a great gap between rich and poor.

### *The problem with agriculture…*

The October Revolution left the communist revolutionaries with a problem: Russia was not the kind of country in which most communists had expected a revolution to occur. Instead of being an industrial country, it was rural and agricultural. It had only a small industrial working class, and its farming was very backward. In the countryside, peasants lived traditional lives, with little education, and were very religious. None of this suited communist ideology.

111

Another problem with farming – from the communist point of view – was that it was run by independent peasant farmers. The farmers behaved like capitalists – trying to make more money for themselves, and wanting the government to leave them alone. Under the New Economic Policy (NEP) peasant farmers had gained considerable freedom to run their farms, sell their produce, and make money. More successful farmers could buy land from poorer neighbours, and employ others to work for them. The richest of these farmers were called 'kulaks' in Russian (see page 10). While there was some co-operation in villages on how to organise the local farming, most farmers worked independently – and did as they wished.

The communist government wanted to get rid of this last survival of independence and capitalism, and bring farming under the control of the government and its plans for the country. They especially wanted to get rid of the kulaks – any kulaks who opposed their plans would be removed.

## Other reasons for reforming agriculture

Ideology was not the only reason why Stalin wanted to transform the Soviet Union from a rural and agricultural country to an urban and industrial one.

### The problem of the New Economic Policy (NEP)

In the 1920s, some communists – including Stalin's rival Bukharin – hoped that by allowing greater freedom to peasants, farming would improve and modernise gradually. This would generate wealth that could be invested in industrialising the Soviet Union. This is what the NEP was designed to do. The NEP was also intended to encourage the idea that workers and peasants were allies in the Soviet Union.

### Extend your knowledge

**Peace and harmony**

Bukharin used the Russian word *smychka* ('harmony' or 'alliance') to describe the relationship between workers and peasants. He hoped that the alliance would provide a foundation for sustainable growth in the economy and peace within the Soviet Union.

By the late 1920s, the NEP did not appear to be working. Peasant grain production was falling, and the government faced a crisis: how was it going to get enough grain out of the countryside to feed the cities and pay for new industries? One answer would have been to pay a higher price for grain, and so encourage peasants to produce more. However, many communists were unwilling to do this, as they felt they were being dictated to by the peasants. The NEP had never been popular in the party, and now opposition to it was growing. While the policy had brought some benefits, to many communists – including Stalin – it looked like a failure overall.

**Summary of successes and failures of the NEP from the point of view of the Communist Party.**

| Successes of the NEP | Failures of the NEP |
|---|---|
| More grain was being provided. There were no more food shortages. | It appeared that the kulaks had 'won' and peasants were deciding government policy. |
| The small business sector was growing. | Peasants were making a profit – capitalism seemed to be growing again. |
| There was less peasant unrest (which was a threat to communist rule). | Agriculture was still not being modernised. |
| | Agriculture was still organised around privately-owned farms. |
| | Middle-class managers were running many factories. |
| | Industrialisation was happening too slowly. |

### The war scare of 1927

In 1927, the Soviet Union was gripped by fear of a war breaking out with neighbouring anti-communist countries. There was tension with Poland in the west, and Japan and China to the east. There was, in fact, little danger of war breaking out at this time; but the fear of war caused many in the communist leadership to worry about how they would feed the Red Army and the people in the towns and cities, if a war did break out. They decided that they needed to get control of agriculture, and force more grain out of the peasants.

### The power struggle

Stalin's last rival in the power struggle (see Section 3.1) was Bukharin. Bukharin supported the NEP and the idea of co-operating with the peasants. By abandoning the NEP, and taking on the peasants, Stalin could isolate Bukharin and complete his own steps to power.

### Source A

From a speech by Stalin, given in December 1929.

```
To launch an offensive against the kulaks
means that we must smash the kulaks,
eliminate them as a class. Unless we set
ourselves these aims, an offensive would be
a mere declamation [lip service], pinpricks,
phrase-mongering, anything but a real
Bolshevik offensive. To launch an offensive
against the kulaks means that we must prepare
for it and then strike at the kulaks, strike
so hard as to prevent them from rising to
their feet again.
```

### Activities ?

1 Explain how Russia was different to the kind of country in which a communist revolution was expected to happen.

2 How did the NEP add to this 'problem'? What was the Communist Party's solution to this 'problem'?

# Stalin's solution: collectivisation

Stalin was eager to transform the Soviet Union – as quickly as possible – from a country of peasant farmers into a modern industrial urban society of factories and cities. He wanted to make the country into the kind of place where a communist revolution *should* have happened – he would force reality to fit communist theory.

As part of this change, agriculture needed to become more productive and efficient. Small farms would be combined into larger state-run farms, run according to modern ideas and methods, and equipped with modern machinery. This was the policy known as collectivisation.

Only in this way could agriculture support the wider aims of the state. Modernised collective farms would generate enough produce to feed the growing cities and the Red Army, and surplus produce could be sold abroad to pay for new industrial machinery. There was much support for this within the Communist Party, and among most workers.

Some historians think that – given time – the NEP might have succeeded in building up the economy of the Soviet Union and gradually paying for industrialisation. But Stalin was too impatient to give the NEP time to do this. Also, he was unhappy at the freedom that the NEP was giving peasants. The positive achievements of the NEP were not enough to make up for the things that Stalin – and many others in the Communist Party – disliked about it.

## The organisation of collective farms

Stalin and the leadership of the Communist Party believed that the way forward was the collectivisation of agriculture. All peasants should join what were called 'collective farms' ('kolkhoz' in Russian). On the kolkhozes the peasants would work together, share land and equipment, and produce grain and other farm produce according to targets set by the government. Profits would be distributed among the members of the kolkhoz – but only after all the demands of the state had been met. If the demand was high – there would be little left.

There would also be another type of community called a 'state farm' ('sovkhoz' in Russian). A sovkhoz usually had much more land than a kolkhoz. The peasants who worked the fields and looked after livestock on a sovkhoz were paid a wage by the government. This fixed wage gave them a better income than members of the kolkhozes.

Most peasants in the Soviet Union ended up in a kolkhoz. In theory, they did so because they volunteered. In reality – things were very different.

## Source B

Official Soviet photograph showing peasants voluntarily voting to join a collective farm in the winter of 1929–30.

### The drive to collectivise

The government needed to sell grain abroad in order to industrialise the Soviet Union. However, they were unwilling to pay peasants more in order to persuade them to grow more. In fact, from 1926, the price paid to peasants for grain went down. As a result, peasants cut back on the amount of grain they were producing or hoarded* it, in the hope that the price would rise later. This was a problem that the communist government had created for the country, but to them it looked as if peasants were to blame. The communist government and the peasants were on a head-on collision course.

## Key term

**Hoarded***

Kept in storage, rather than selling it on.

In the winter of 1927–28, the grain shortages were so bad that Stalin led a campaign of force to seize grain from peasants. This became known as the 'Urals-Siberian method'. The NEP was dead.

### The 'liquidation of the kulaks'

The next step took place in the winter of 1928–29, when peasants were forced to join kolkhozes. Those who resisted were denounced as kulaks and arrested.

In December 1929, Stalin launched a campaign to liquidate* the kulaks. Only around 2% of peasants were actually wealthy enough to employ other peasants – but the definition of 'kulak' soon stretched to anyone who refused to join a collective farm in the winter of 1929–30.

## Key term

**Liquidate***

To get rid of: some were arrested, some had their property taken away, others were killed.

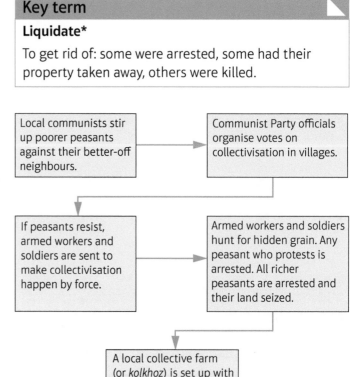

**Figure 4.1** How collectivisation was carried out.

Those defined as 'kulaks' suffered terribly. About 30,000 were killed in 1930–31 – most were shot on the spot. Others were taken away from their homes. Of these, about two million were transported to the arctic north and to Siberia. There, huge numbers were worked to death, or died from the cold and poor food. Some survived, and were released in the mid-1930s – only to be shot later, in 1937, when the secret police were ordered to remove surviving 'enemies of the people' (see Source A, Chapter 3.2). Many others were exiled to areas closer to their homes, but often onto land that was very difficult to farm, and where survival was almost impossible.

For Stalin, this was the completion of the revolution in the countryside. It was about more than seizing grain and reorganising agriculture – important as that was.

It was also about stamping the control of the Communist Party onto the peasant population – and crushing all who resisted. It was about power and politics – as well as about farming and the economy with 'Co-operation'.

## Source C

An official poster from the 1920s showing a peasant smashing 'Private Trade' and a 'Kulak Parasite'.

## Opposition to collectivisation

Despite government claims that most peasants supported the move to collective farms, the reality was that both rich and poor peasants resented the government interfering in their lives. The official propaganda claimed that it was just the kulaks who opposed collectivisation, but in fact most of the rural population opposed what the communists were doing.

## Activities

1. Read Source A. Explain Stalin's aim in launching collectivisation.

2. Explain how photographs, such as Source B, and posters, such as Source B on page 95, helped him communicate his view of why and how collectivisation was to be carried out. What message was each of them designed to get across?

3. Does the evidence support Stalin's view that the problems in Soviet agriculture were caused by a minority of kulaks holding the country to ransom in order to increase prices? Use information from this section to write a short paragraph about this.

## Extend your knowledge

### Letters of complaint

We know a lot about how peasants felt about collectivisation because many wrote letters of complaint to their local Communist Party. When the German army invaded the Soviet Union in 1941, the party records in Smolensk were seized and taken back to Germany. In 1945, the American army captured the papers and took them to the USA, where they have been studied by historians investigating collectivisation.

Many peasants chose to destroy crops and livestock rather than hand them over to the communists. Vast numbers of animals were destroyed.

The countryside was spiralling into chaos.

In 1930, Stalin halted the collectivisation campaign. He made a speech in which he accused Communist Party officials of being 'dizzy with success'. He claimed that they were going beyond their orders when they forced peasants to join collective farms. This was a lie – but it did the trick. The collectivisation campaign slowed down; huge numbers of peasants left the collective farms; and work began to prepare crops for the harvest.

But then Stalin struck again.

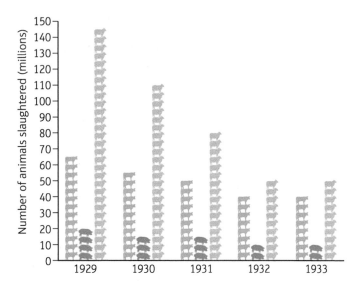

**Figure 4.2** Numbers of animals slaughtered in the Soviet Union, 1929–33.

## The completion of the campaign

In 1932–33, the collectivisation campaign began once more. As it was completed, an appalling famine struck the Soviet Union. Millions died as a result of the upheavals, deportations and government grain seizures – which still went ahead even though people were starving. In Kazakhstan about 1.3 million people starved to death and about one million died in Russia. Even more died in the Ukraine. Across the Soviet Union, as a whole, about 5.7 million people died during collectivisation . Some historians think that the total number of deaths could have been as high as seven million.

By July 1933, 83% of all arable* land and 64% of all peasant households had been collectivised. Most of the rest were brought into the system as the 1930s progressed. The Communist Party was finally in control of the countryside; but this had been achieved at an incredibly high price – in terms of human lives, destruction of livestock, and loss of personal freedom.

| Key term |
| --- |
| **Arable*** |
| Producing crops such as wheat and barley. |

## Mechanisation – the Machine Tractor Stations (MTS)

As part of the attempt to modernise farming methods, Machine Tractor Stations (MTSs) were set up to rent out agricultural machinery (such as tractors and combine harvesters) to groups of collective farms. The MTSs also acted as collecting points for the grain being demanded by the state.

Each MTS also had a 'political department' – staffed by members of the secret police – to keep a watch on local communities. There was often confusion over who was running the kolkhozes: the collective farm managers, local Communist Party bosses, or the MTS staff.

In many areas, there were not enough tractors to go round; and collective farms continued to rely on traditional methods, like harvesting by hand and ploughing with horse-drawn ploughs.

## Famine in the Ukraine: the *'Holodomor'*

In the south of the Soviet Union lay the Ukraine. Today it is an independent country, but in the 1930s it was part of the Soviet Union. The Red Army had defeated Ukrainian nationalists during the Russian Civil War, which prevented Ukraine from breaking away to become an independent state – in the way that Finland, Latvia, Lithuania, and Russian-ruled Poland had done. Ukraine was a large and valuable asset for the Soviet Union – and has been described as the 'bread basket' of the Soviet Union – because its farms produced such large amounts of grain.

Many Ukrainian peasants refused to join the collective farms. To them it felt like going back to the times of serfdom*. They had no intention of giving up their freedom and independence – but armed workers, the secret police, and the Red Army, forced peasants to join collective farms, and 'liquidated' anyone classed as a kulak. The suffering was worse in the Ukraine than elsewhere in the Soviet Union. This was partly because its

| Key term |
| --- |
| **Serfdom*** |
| Being a serf. Serfs were peasants who were owned by their landlords. All peasants in the tsarist Russian empire were serfs until 1861. |

population contained so many peasant families – but also because Stalin's government was determined to smash Ukrainian independence and national culture finally.

More and more grain was taken from Ukraine – even as people were starving. Starving people resorted to cannibalism – eating corpses. Some parents went mad with hunger, and killed and ate their own children. Desperate peasants flooded into cities in search of food. The police arrested thousands of starving orphan children and left them to die in prison. At the same time, many Ukrainian religious and political leaders were executed. Others died later in the Great Terror after 1936.

In Ukraine, this time of starvation is remembered as the 'Holodomor'. In the Ukrainian language this means 'extermination by hunger'. Between 1932 and 1933, huge numbers died in one of the largest deliberate famines in human history. Stalin's government denied it was happening, refused foreign aid, and kept the famine going. It has been estimated that during June 1933, 28,000 people died from hunger every day.

It is difficult to be sure of exactly how many died in the Holodomor overall; but modern estimates suggest it was about 3.3 million, of which about 3 million were Ukrainians, and the rest other ethnic groups living in Ukraine. Millions of Ukrainians also died of famine in other areas of the Soviet Union. The number of Ukrainians who died during collectivisation was more than any other nationality in the Soviet Union.

## Source D

A Ukrainian children's song from the time of the Holodomor.

```
Father Stalin, look at this
Collective farming is just bliss
The hut's in ruins, the barn's all sagged
All the horses broken nags
And on the hut a hammer and sickle
And in the hut death and famine
No cows left, no pigs at all
Just your picture on the wall
Daddy and mommy are in the kolkhoz
The poor child cries as alone he goes
There's no bread and there's no fat
The party's ended all of that
Seek not the gentle nor the mild
A father's eaten his own child
The party man he beats and stamps
And sends us to Siberian camps.
```

## Source E

From an interview with a survivor of the Holodomor, Antonina Meleshchenko, from the village of Kosivka, Ukraine.

```
The famine began. People were eating cats,
dogs, in the Ros' river all the frogs were
caught [and eaten]. Children were gathering
insects in the fields and died... Stronger
peasants were forced to collect the dead to
the cemeteries; they were stacked on the
carts like firewood, then dropped off into
one big pit. The dead were all around: on
the roads, near the river, by the fences. I
used to have five brothers. Altogether 792
have died in our village during the famine,
in the [Second World War], 135.
```

## Interpretation 1

From Socialist Planning, by M. Ellman, published in 2014.

The collectivisation of agriculture in the USSR also provided a substantial increase in the urban labour force. The mass deportations from the villages, and the mass arrests, together with the sharp drop in animal products and grain supplies... severely depressed rural living standards and drove millions of villagers to the towns.

## Source F

An unofficial photograph taken by a bystander of starving peasants lying on a Ukrainian street in 1933.

117

## THINKING HISTORICALLY — Interpretations (4b)

### Method is everything

A spectrum of historical methodology

**Bad history**
- Based on gut feeling
- Argument does not progress logically
- No supporting evidence

**Good history**
- Based on an interpretation of evidence
- Argument progresses logically
- Evidence used to support argument

### Student conclusion 1

"I think that Stalin launched the 'liquidation of the kulaks' in 1929 because they were standing in the way of his plans to transform agriculture in the USSR, to secure food supplies for the cities and the Red Army, and finally to get rid of capitalism in the countryside. Kulaks were opposed to the communist plans for agriculture and so Stalin removed them."

### Student conclusion 2

"The decision to 'liquidate the kulaks', that started in 1929, came after grain shortages in 1927–28 which caused problems in food supplies to the cities. As well as this, there was a war scare in 1927 and the Soviet leadership feared they could not guarantee food supplies in time of war. On top of that, the USSR was well behind other countries in terms of industrialisation and needed to increase agricultural production in order to sell grain abroad. For these reasons Stalin launched collectivisation and the removal of the kulaks."

### Student conclusion 3

"On one hand the Soviet leadership feared that, as long as farming was run by the peasants, there would be a danger of them holding back grain in order to push up prices; and kulaks growing wealthy meant that capitalist ideas would continue to influence the USSR. There was evidence to support this fear in the grain shortages of 1927–28, when peasants held back grain, and in the fact that the NEP had reduced government control over peasants and trade. For this reason, Stalin decided to remove kulaks and bring agriculture under state control.

However, the situation was more complex. The government itself was largely to blame for grain shortages because it cut prices paid for grain in 1926, and ignored the fact that rich and poor peasants opposed collectivisation. The decision in 1929 to 'liquidate the kulaks' was driven by Stalin's desire to crush all peasants, punish the Ukraine, undermine Bukharin (who supported an alliance with the peasants) and increase his personal support among Communist Party members and workers. He used the claim that kulaks were opposing the government as an excuse to launch a war against all the peasants."

Work in pairs. Read the above conclusions and answer the questions.

1  Look at all the conclusions. In what ways do they differ from one another?
2  Look carefully at the spectrum of historical methodology.
   a  Where would you place each student's conclusion on the spectrum?
   b  What evidence would you use to support your choice?
   c  Suggest one improvement to each conclusion that would move it towards 'good' historical writing.
3  How important is it that we know what to look for when we are reading and evaluating historical writing?

## Activities ?

1   What can you infer from Source D about children's view of collectivisation?

2   Use Sources E and F to explain why such a song was sung in the Ukraine.

3   'Collectivisation was terrible, and yet it also assisted industrialisation'. Using Interpretation 1 and other information, explain how far you agree with this view.

## Successes and failures of collectivisation

### Successes...

- The Communist Party was now in control of the countryside – a political success for Stalin.
- Each Machine Tractor Station (MTS) had a member of the secret police to keep watch on the area – this increased the government's control over the population.
- Grain sold abroad helped pay for the Five-Year Plans – an economic success for Stalin.
- Huge numbers of peasants fled to cities where they became workers in the new factories built during the Five-Year Plans. About 19 million people were on the move – a vast number.

### Failures...

- Huge numbers of people died – a terrible human tragedy.
- Food supplies were disrupted by the chaos in the countryside.
- Living standards in towns and countryside fell.
- There were too few tractors, and agriculture remained backwards.
- Many of the most experienced and capable peasant farmers were killed.
- Agriculture in the Soviet Union took years to recover, and some historians think it remained inefficient right through to the end of communist rule.

## Summary

- The communists distrusted the peasants and wanted to bring them under state control.
- They felt that the NEP was benefitting peasants at the expense of industrialisation.
- In order to change this, they collectivised agriculture and 'liquidated the kulaks'.
- The grain seized helped pay for the Five-Year Plans – but at a terrible cost in human lives.

## Checkpoint

### Strengthen

**S1** Create a spidergram of the causes of collectivisation. Underline what you consider to be the most important cause and explain why you chose it.

**S2** Create a spidergram of the consequences of collectivisation. Underline what you consider to be the most important consequence and explain why you chose it.

### Challenge

Work on these tasks in small groups:

**C1**  'The slogan "liquidation of the kulaks" was a piece of communist propaganda that had no link to the reality of what was really happening in the countryside'. Say whether you agree or disagree with this interpretation and why.

**C2** Make a note of the effects of collectivisation under these headings: Economic effects, Political effects, Social effects.

How confident do you feel about your answers to these questions? Compare your answers with another group. Add to or edit your answers as a result of this larger group discussion.

# 4.2 Changes in industry

## Learning outcomes

- Understand why industrialisation was important to Stalin.
- Understand why the Five-Year Plans were put in place.
- Know about the mixed results of the Five-Year Plans.

## Stalin's motives for rapid industrialisation

As we have seen, Stalin had strong ideological reasons for rapidly industrialising the Soviet Union. A country of mines, steelworks, factories, roads and locomotives running on newly-built railways, was what the Communist Party wanted for the country.

### Extend your knowledge

#### Stalin's nickname

Stalin's real name was Joseph Vissarionovich Dzhugashvili. 'Stalin' was his nickname: which means 'man of steel'. He started using this alternative name before 1914. It later turned out to be doubly appropriate: he was a hard man and, also, under him the iron and steel production in the Soviet Union increased enormously.

### Problems of the New Economic Policy (NEP)

At the same time as problems were occurring in agricultural production, industrial production was also failing to increase with sufficient speed. The 'scissors crisis' (see page 68) suggested that the NEP was never going to be able to pay for industrialisation at the pace the communist leadership wanted. If Stalin had been willing to compromise with the peasants – by allowing more time for the economy to grow – this might have turned out differently.

### The war scare of 1927

The war scare caused serious concerns about industry as well as agriculture (see page 110). If the Soviet Union found itself involved in a modern war, then it would need an industrial sector capable of producing weapons, planes, bombs and tanks – in vast numbers. This would involve coal and iron mining, oil production, chemical works and steel-making – as well as factories capable of making the finished weapons. The quicker the Soviet Union industrialised the better. It was a matter of national security – even of national survival.

### The power struggle

During the power struggle (see Section 3.1), first Trotsky, and then Zinoviev and Kamenev, had criticised the slow pace of industrialisation. By taking up this idea, and driving the Soviet Union forward himself, Stalin could undermine any support these rivals had in the Communist Party. This tactic also made it more likely that, once these rivals had been defeated, their followers would fall in line with the new leadership under Stalin.

### Encouraging worker enthusiasm for communist policies

The Communist Party looked to workers for its most enthusiastic support. After all, it claimed to be the party of the working class (see Section 1.1 and 4.1). By abandoning the NEP, and building new industries, it was giving a clear signal that it was industrial workers who represented the future of the Soviet Union.

In encouraging a new generation of young working-class people to build a new modern country, the Communist Party was also looking to increase support for itself and its plans. Young workers soon embraced the changes with great enthusiasm and commitment.

## Source A

A poster showing new working opportunities for young women, issued in 1932.

## Interpretation 1

From *An Economic History of the USSR*, by A. Nove, published in 1989.

*Many young communists found great satisfaction in living hard in tents and huts, building the great factories which would change Russia and make a happy future for generations to come. Stalin himself was no romantic but saw advantages in harnessing such feelings as these.*

*Vast new industries were not created merely by threats. It must again be emphasised that we have been describing a system in which, despite the terror, many devoted people worked hard for the Cause, or for Russia, or even for their own advancement, but worked with a will.*

## Competition with the West

After the Wall Street Crash of October 1929, western countries faced huge economic difficulties. They cut back on spending, and unemployment rose dramatically. In contrast, Stalin decided on economic growth to make the Soviet Union seem a place of energy, expansion and change – so that communism, not capitalism, would offer hope for the future.

# An industrial war: 'There is no fortress that a communist cannot storm…'

In 1926, the Communist Party Congress decided to embark on a huge drive to industrialise the Soviet Union. In 1927, a Five-Year Plan was prepared to begin this leap forward. It was a time of tremendous excitement, and a sense of confidence, among all those who believed in the victory of communism in the Soviet Union. It was like a war – with heroes and heroines, fronts and battles, casualties and victories. Only this 'war' was an economic war – its battles were the production targets for steel, coal and tractors. For many young communist workers this was a time of great sacrifice – but also the most exciting time of their lives! They were soldiers on an industrial front. They were confident. They believed in the slogan: 'There is no fortress that a communist cannot storm'. They would transform and modernise the Soviet Union.

## The work of Gosplan

'Gosplan' was the State Planning Committee. Its job was to take the general aims of the communist leadership and turn these into specific goals for key industries to meet. The first state planning organisation had originally been set up in 1920; and in 1923 it was given the job of co-ordinating the industrial plans of the different soviet republics.

Once the decision was taken to launch Five-Year Plans, it became immensely important. From 1928, it was Gosplan that set and supervised the targets that factory managers and workers had to achieve across the whole of the Soviet Union. Under Gosplan, five thousand new factories were established between 1928 and 1937.

## The Five-Year Plans

The Communist Party was determined that it could modernise the Soviet Union at rapid speed – and it set out detailed plans as to how this was to be done. These were known as the Five-Year Plans. Each plan set targets for different industries. Tremendous pressure was put on managers and workers to meet these targets and, as a result of this, the First and Second Five-Year Plans were each completed in just **four** years.

### Timeline

**The Five-Year Plans**

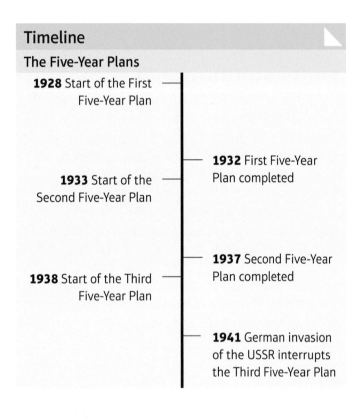

**1928** Start of the First Five-Year Plan

**1932** First Five-Year Plan completed

**1933** Start of the Second Five-Year Plan

**1937** Second Five-Year Plan completed

**1938** Start of the Third Five-Year Plan

**1941** German invasion of the USSR interrupts the Third Five-Year Plan

### Source B

The Soviet newspaper *Pravda*, in May 1929, on the aims of the First Five-Year Plan.

```
Before our eyes we saw our country as it will
be in five years' time. Exciting prospect!
As if by some magic hand the curtains which
conceal the future have been parted!
```

### Activity                                                    ?

Design a poster to be published in the Soviet Union in 1929, to explain the need for the Five-Year Plans. Try to communicate both the excitement of the idea, and the urgent need for it. Use Sources A and B and Interpretation 1 to assist you.

### Exam-style question, Section A                              ●

Explain why Stalin launched the Five-Year Plans. You may use the following:

- the NEP
- Soviet industry

You **must** also use information of your own. **12 marks**

### Exam tip                                                    ●

Explain why each of the factors given played a part in Stalin's decision-making. Add more reasons: for example, the state of the world in the late-1920s and the 1930s. In conclusion, state which you think was the most important reason and why.

---

**First Five-Year Plan (1928–32)**
Increase output of 'heavy industries' such as coal, iron, steel, engineering and chemicals.

**Second Five-Year Plan (1933–37)**
Increase output of 'heavy industries' such as coal, iron, steel, engineering and chemicals.
Greater efficiency and better use of resources.
Make some consumer goods.

**Third Five-Year Plan (1938–41)**
Improvements to education.
Make more military equipment.

**Figure 4.3** The aims of the Five-Year Plans, 1928–1941. The first two plans were each completed in four years. The third was cut short when Hitler invaded in 1941.

# The Stakhanovite Movement

Aleksey Stakhanov was the son of a peasant who worked in the coal mines of eastern Ukraine. It was reported that, on the night of 31 August 1935, he had mined a record 102 tonnes of coal in less than six hours – 14 times his quota! This started the 'Stakhanovite Movement' – workers across the Soviet Union were encouraged to copy Stakhanov and over-fulfil targets.

Stakhanov became a national hero, travelling the country and addressing meetings. He was so famous, he even appeared on the cover of *Time* magazine in the USA. He went on to study at the Industrial Academy in Moscow. After this, he became the head of a coal mine in Kazakhstan in 1941. Later, he worked at the Ministry of Coal. He was awarded some of the Soviet Union's top honours, including: two Orders of Lenin, the Order of the Red Banner, and many other medals.

In fact, the whole thing was a set-up. Unlike other miners, Stakhanov had assistants, and equipment in good working order. Over time, many workers came to resent the Stakhanovites; and, in Russian, the word *Stakhanovets* came to mean a pushy person who was more interested in helping themselves than worrying about the problems this caused for others. Mine and factory managers spent much time dealing with Stakhanovites who, far from helping move industry forwards, were actually a cause of disruption – because they only cared about their own productivity, and not how their behaviour affected the rest of the workplace.

However, the government was keen to promote the Stakhanovite Movement; and many factory managers later lost their lives in the Great Terror for blocking the demands of Stakhanovites. The managers were accused of being wreckers – holding back Soviet progress.

## Source C

Photograph of Vasili Kochetov – a Stakhanovite – with fellow coal miners at the Tula coal fields in the 1930s.

## Source D

From a conversation between N.I. Mashurov, mine supervisor, and Stakhanov, in August 1935, recorded in Stakhanov's memoirs.

```
There will be air [compressed air to power
the drill], there will be wood [for props to
hold up the roof of the tunnel]. How much you
squeeze out, we will see. I guarantee over a
hundred tons. It will be a record.
```

## Source E

Data about Aleksey Stakhanov's achievement in 1935, found in Soviet sources from the time.

| Characteristics | Usual mining shift | Stakhanov's shift |
|---|---|---|
| Time of day of shift | Day time | Night time |
| Length of shift | 5 hours and 45 minutes | 5 hours and 45 minutes |
| Numbers of miners at coal face | 8 | 1 |
| Seams (ledges) of coal available to cut per miner | 1 | 8 |
| Numbers of helpers per miner | 0 | 2 |
| Target of coal to be dug per miner | 6.5 tons | 6.5 tons |
| Amount of coal dug per shift at one coal face | 52 tons | 102 tons |

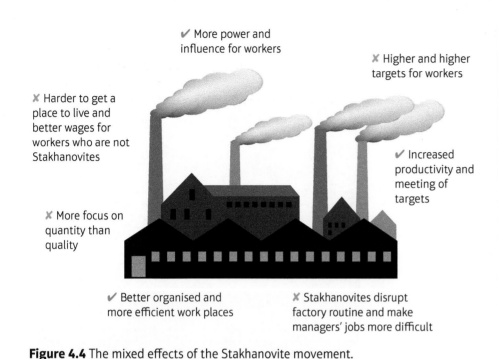

**Figure 4.4** The mixed effects of the Stakhanovite movement.

## Activities ?

Discuss the following questions in a small group, and share your conclusions with the rest of the class:

1   Why did the Soviet government publish photographs such as Source C?

2   Why was the Stakhanovite Movement an important part of the Five-Year Plans?

3   Explain how the Stakhanovite Movement had both positive and negative effects.

---

**THINKING HISTORICALLY** ▸ **Evidence (4a&b)**

### The 'weight' of evidence

One useful idea to have in mind when interpreting historical sources is 'consistency' – whether or not sources support each other. If a number of sources appear to suggest the same conclusion about the past, then we might feel more confident about accepting this conclusion.

However, we should also consider the nature of the sources and the reasons why sources might seem to disagree.

Sources D and E could be used by a historian to build up a picture of just how remarkable the achievement of Stakhanov was.

1   Explain how Sources D and E differ in what they suggest about Stakhanov's achievement.

2   How can the different suggestions found in these sources be explained? Write down as many reasons as you can.

Discuss the following in groups:

3   Suppose a historian had ten more accounts that agreed broadly with Source D and only four that agreed with Source E. Would this mean that Source D was nearer to the truth? Explain your answer.

4   What else should we consider, apart from 'the balance of the evidence', when drawing conclusions from sources such as these?

## Successes and failures of industrialisation

### Successes...

- There was huge increase in output under the First Five-Year Plan; some increased efficiency under the Second Five-Year Plan; and a great increase in the amount of military equipment produced under the Third Five-Year Plan.

- There was a massive growth in heavy industry. In new industrial cities – such as Magnitogorsk, Komsomolsk and Novosibirsk – massive new steelworks and industrial complexes produced a vast output of modern material and goods. The biggest dam in Europe was built on the river Dnieper; and there was a huge expansion of the railway network.

- Unemployment (which had been 1.3 million in 1928) vanished. Everyone had a job.

- Supplies of raw materials went up. Coal production increased massively.

- Re-armament was also a huge achievement. Weapons that would eventually help the Soviet Union win the Second World War were made in the factories of the Five-Year Plans.

- There was great enthusiasm among workers. Many thousands of young adults volunteered to build cities such as Magnitogorsk – living in tents, in freezing conditions, to build the blast furnaces. Others worked underground to build the Moscow Metro. For these young people, the 1930s were a purposeful and exciting time.

- For the Communist Party, the huge increase in the numbers of workers meant that it had more allies than when the Soviet Union had been a largely peasant country. In 1928, there were approximately 4.6 million industrial workers in the Soviet Union – by 1940 this had risen to 12.6 million.

- Industry spread to areas east of the Ural Mountains that had never previously been industrialised. New factories were built in Siberia and East Asia.

### Activity ?

For many young Russians the Five-Year Plans were the most exciting period of their lives. Imagine you are writing a letter home from Magnitogorsk to relatives in your village, in 1936. Explain why you feel so positive about what you have achieved.

### Source F

Soviet poster from 1930, showing how the factories of the Five-Year Plans will help defend the Soviet Union. The green figures represent Nazism, Christianity and 'slander'.

### Extend your knowledge

**Beyond the bombers**

When the Second World War came to the Soviet Union, in 1941, the factories built east of the Ural Mountains, during the Five-Year Plans, were out of range of German bomber aircraft, so could continue to produce vast numbers of tanks and other weapons. This helped the Soviet Union to defeat Nazi Germany.

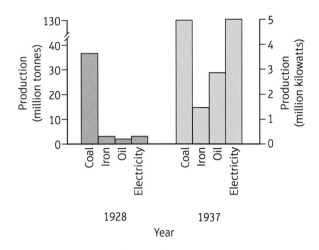

**Figure 4.5** Industrial output in the Soviet Union in 1928 (at the start of the First Five-Year Plan) and 1937 (at the end of the Second Five-Year Plan).

## Failures...

- The First Five-Year Plan stressed output over the quality of the goods produced. The Soviet Union remained inefficient and wasteful despite the Second Five-Year Plan.

- Low quality goods were a great problem: tyres blew after short distances, machines broke down. The preference for meeting targets – rather than making high quality goods – continued to be a problem for as long as the Soviet Union remained a communist country.

- Compared to factories in other countries, productivity was still low. For example, workers in the Soviet Union produced far less than workers in comparable factories in the USA.

- There were terrible shortages of consumer goods, and workers' standards of living were low (see Section 4.3). People had to queue for hours for basic items such as shoes and clothes.

- Production techniques were wasteful and inefficient. All that mattered was that the job got done – and that workers and managers avoided blame for any failures! As a result, work was often done using more resources, and with more waste and confusion, than in the better-run factories of Germany or the USA – where profit was a key factor, and waste cost money.

- Health and safety at work was terrible. There was little concern about the safety of workers – huge numbers of people fell from scaffolding, were crushed by machinery, or froze to death.

- Organisation and transport was often chaotic. Things did not arrive in the correct places; machinery and other items were left out in freezing winter weather and ruined.

- Claims made regarding the numbers of items produced could not be trusted. Factory managers produced false figures to protect themselves from being arrested as wreckers, who were accused of not fulfilling their targets in the plan.

## Source G

From a memoir by Ivanov, the first director of the Stalingrad tractor factory, describing the early days of production in 1930.

In the assembly shop I talked to a young man who was grinding sockets. I asked him how he measured and he showed me how he used his fingers. We had no measuring instruments!

## Source H

From an article by P. Sinitsyn, published in the Soviet magazine *Novy Mir* in 1967, discussing the building of the Stalingrad tractor factory in 1930.

Remember how this industry was created, which now produces the largest number of tractors in the world, how and in what conditions the first great tractor-works in the country was built in a year and working to full capacity a year later. All this was done in a country where as late as 1910 over two thirds of the ploughs were wooden.

## Interpretation 2

From *The Russian Revolution, 1900–1927*, by R. Service, published in 1991.

*The early Five-Year Plans catapulted the USSR in the direction of full industrial modernisation and the potentiality for the defeat of a mighty aggressor such as Nazi Germany... But forced rate industrialisation and forcible agricultural collectivisation caused horrendous and unjustifiable social torment. Stalin, moreover, claimed too much! He ignored the progress already made in the later imperial and early Soviet [NEP] epochs; industrialisation was in motion before his political ascendancy [rise to power] commenced.*

## Summary

- The communists believed it was vital to industrialise the Soviet Union – and to do it quickly.
- The decision to do this also strengthened Stalin's political control.
- In ten years, the Soviet Union made changes that had taken a century in other countries.
- This achievement also had negative effects on the economy and society of the Soviet Union.

## Checkpoint

### Strengthen

**S1** Create a spidergram to explain why Stalin launched the Five-Year Plans. Underline the most important cause, in your opinion, and explain why you chose this one.

**S2** Create a spidergram showing the consequences of the Five-Year Plans. Underline the most important consequence, in your opinion, and explain why you chose this one.

### Challenge

**C1** 'The Stakhanovites were more trouble than they were worth in the building of the economy of the USSR'. Explain whether you agree or disagree and why.

**C2** Discuss this statement: 'Stalin's decision to launch the Five-Year Plans made the USSR into a modern state'.

**C3** In pairs, create a poster representing your thoughts on C2. Display the posters around the classroom. Review each other's posters, and comment on their strengths and areas for improvement.

How confident do you feel about your answers to these questions? Review your answers with a partner. If you are still uncertain about the answers ask your teacher for help.

# 4.3 Life in the Soviet Union in the 1930s

## Learning outcomes

- Know about the living and working conditions experienced in the Soviet Union in the 1930s.
- Understand why some groups in society enjoyed better lifestyles than others.
- Know how conditions differed for workers and peasants – and for men and women.

In theory, the Soviet Union was a classless society, in which nobody was treated better or worse because of their social background or position. In practice, there were big differences in the quality of life on offer. Internal passports, issued from 1932, identified people by their class, job, and ethnic and social background. People from groups regarded as 'desirable' by the government – for example industrial workers – could get better jobs and housing. Those from a less desirable background – such as rich peasants and ex-aristocrats – found life much harder. However, even among those people regarded as desirable, there were big differences in the quality of life.

For the vast majority – the peasants and workers – living and working standards were low; but, in some respects, life was better for workers, and worse for peasants. Urban workers received higher pay and access to more food and goods. Many peasants remained unhappy with life on the collective farms – and internal passports were introduced partly in order to restrict their movement.

## Living and working conditions for workers in the towns

### Housing
Housing, for many who lived in towns and cities, was low quality. Many workers lived in barracks, with little comfort and few conveniences. Better-off worker families might have a small flat with communal (shared) kitchens and toilets.

### Food and clothing
Food was in short supply. Between 1928 and 1933, the consumption of meat, fruit and milk in the city of Leningrad declined by 66%. Food rationing officially ended in 1935, but there was still not enough – and queuing to get food became an everyday experience for most people in the Soviet Union in the 1930s.

Consumer goods were few. The Five-Year Plans were focused on heavy industry and transportation; so many basic necessities – such as shoes and clothing – were in short supply. More luxurious items – like watches and radios – were even harder to come by.

### Working conditions
Working conditions were hard. In 1932 the law was changed, so that if a worker had one day off work – without a 'good reason' – they lost their job, housing and ration card. By 1940, being 20 minutes late to work led to a 25% cut in pay for six months! Health and safety at work was limited – and there were many accidents.

Stalin reintroduced major differences between workers, depending on their productivity. Earlier communist ideas about equality of wages were abandoned. Workers had to compete with each other for better pay and conditions.

### Personal rights
Personal freedom was limited. The government introduced internal passports in 1932, in an attempt to try to prevent people from freely moving around the country, looking for a new job. By the end of 1934, over 27 million internal passports had been issued. The police could ask to see a person's internal passport at any time; and if it didn't show they had the 'right' to be in that city, or workplace, they could be arrested and imprisoned.

## Extend your knowledge

### Prized possessions

In the industrial city of Magnitogorsk, in the 1930s, even little luxuries – like spoons – were rare. When some were finally made, for the workers' canteen, they were introduced with celebratory speeches and music playing – but the workers stole them all, because they had none at home!

## Source A

A statement on living conditions in the Soviet Union, made by Stalin in January 1933.

```
The material conditions of the workers and
peasants are improving from year to year. The
only ones who can have doubts on this score
are the sworn enemies of the Soviet regime.
```

## Interpretation 1

From *Popular Opinion in Stalin's Russia*, by S. Davies, published in 1997.

*Workers were acutely aware of fluctuations in their standard of living, frequently comparing prices with wages. It was patently obvious to them whether their own economic situation was improving or deteriorating, and they were not deceived by official rhetoric [claims] about rising standards. The rhetoric simply highlighted the disparity [difference] between the fictitious 'good life' and their actual situation. Their personal experience of the Soviet economy, with its queues and deficits [shortages], led to criticism of the regime's refusal to address such issues publicly.*

## Interpretation 2

From *An Economic History of the USSR*, by A. Nove, published in 1989.

*Shortages of consumers' goods... could be attributed to malevolent [ill-willed] plotting by enemies of the people, in the pay of Hitler... and 'Judas-Trotsky'. Thus the shortage of eggs was supposedly due to the efforts of wreckers, who smashed eggs in transit just to deprive the Soviet people of the fruits of their labour and to create politically exploitable discontent. Or so the readers of Pravda [the official newspaper of the Communist Party] were supposed to believe.*

## Activities ?

1 Why did Stalin make the claim that he did in Source A; and *Pravda* make the claims described in Interpretation 2?

2 What does Interpretation 1 suggest about how successful Stalin was in getting his view across to ordinary people in the Soviet Union?

3 Does the evidence support the view in Interpretation 1 – that there was a big difference between Stalin's claims and the realities of everyday life?

# Living and working conditions for peasants in the countryside

### Housing

Villages had always had very basic housing, with outside toilets and water drawn from wells. This continued under the collective farms, with little money going into improving living conditions in the 1930s.

### Food

As in the towns, there was food rationing. Although peasants were producing the food, they didn't get as much to eat as town workers – because they were regarded as being less important. The maximum amount of food was taken from the countryside to feed the growing cities.

### Working conditions

Life at work was hard. There were few tractors or other agricultural machinery – despite official claims – and peasants worked long hours, doing hard physical work, with little reward.

### Personal freedom

Peasants greatly resented losing control over their land, and having to follow the orders of the chairman of the collective farm, who also set productivity targets. They worked slowly, and had little incentive to be efficient. Productivity was so bad that, in 1939, the government was forced to allow peasants to sell produce from their garden plots (and keep the money earned) in order to increase the amount of food available. Soon, just 3% of the land of the collective farms was producing 30% of the food consumed in the Soviet Union. The peasants were capable of being highly productive – when they were allowed freedom to work in their own way, and keep what they earned.

It was illegal for peasants to leave the collective farms and, just like city workers, they were issued internal passports to control their movements. Nonetheless, many ran away to work in towns and cities where they risked being arrested. In the first six months of 1933 alone, 400,000 people were arrested as 'undesirables' and 'socially harmful elements' and imprisoned or deported to other areas. These included prostitutes, beggars and ex-aristocrats – but also huge numbers of ex-kulaks and peasants. Many were dumped in the Urals and western Siberia. Others drifted back to their home areas and lived using forged papers – often helped by factory managers who were desperate for workers. This increased the government's fear of 'hidden enemies'.

## Extend your knowledge

### Peasant pay

The income of a peasant working on a collective farm was about 20% of the average industrial wage in a factory. It is hardly surprising that many peasants ran away to towns and factories where they could find better pay and more personal freedom.

# Living conditions for party officials and members of government

Party officials and members of the government enjoyed a relatively luxurious lifestyle. They had access to shops that ordinary citizens could not use – where they could buy superior clothes, meat, dairy products and even scarce foreign-made goods. This privilege was a way of rewarding their loyalty to the system. It also offered an incentive to others to copy them – in the hope of promotion, and access to their superior lifestyle.

A new ruling class was being set up and rewarded in the officially 'classless' society of the Soviet Union. Its members owed everything to the communist system: education, jobs, lifestyle. In many ways, the new rulers had become more important than the workers. The official explanation was that they held power on behalf of the workers and did what was best for them.

Those who had made it to positions of power by 1940, often blocked other, younger people from competing for their positions. The new communist ruling class wanted to keep its new-found power and privileges. However, people in important positions were also very vulnerable. If they failed to deliver the targets demanded of them, then it could cost them their lives, and could destroy their families too.

## Extend your knowledge

### Official shops

Consumer goods could only be bought at special state-run stores. Workers had to register at these stores before they could shop there. In this way, the government was able to control access to particular goods for different groups of people. The shops that sold the best quality goods were only open to some members of the party and government. This was a way of rewarding loyal followers of Stalin.

## Interpretation 3

From *An Economic History of the USSR*, by A. Nove, published in 1989.

*The period 1929–34 marked a great cataclysm [disaster], which shook the entire society of Russia to its foundations. It was then, facing a dramatic lowering of living standards in towns and coercion in the villages, that the security police secured the dominant place in society that they retained until Stalin's death.*

## Source B

Official Soviet photograph of happy shoppers at a 1930s shop.

# Inequalities between men and women

In both towns and countryside there was lack of gender-equality. The overwhelmingly male communist authorities tended to view female equality as being mostly a question of allowing women access to paid employment in the growing industries. In order to achieve this, most factories had crèche facilities, and women were encouraged to join the industrial workforce.

More far-reaching equality in pay and promotion opportunities was not a priority. As a result, there were many more female workers by 1941 but, on average, they worked for lower pay than men, were rarely promoted to management jobs, and were still expected to juggle work and running the family home.

## Interpretation 4

From *The Great Fear: Stalin's Terror of the 1930s*, by J. Harris, published in 2016.

*For those with more money to spend by virtue of their qualifications or position, especially those living in large urban areas, in key industries and institutions, the improvement in the range of available and affordable foods and consumer goods was felt before long. Stalin was well aware of the political implications of that change. The regime quite deliberately prioritised the distribution system, both to reinforce support among the elite and to encourage productivity in a targeted manner. So, for example, the military, the secret police, and the party elite benefitted disproportionately.*

## Activities ?

1 Interpretation 2 and Interpretation 3 give ways in which Stalin dealt with the dissatisfaction caused by shortages. Explain what these different methods were.

2 According to Interpretation 4, how did Stalin use shortages to increase his power?

3 Does what you know about the Stakhanovite Movement make you inclined to agree or disagree with Interpretation 4?

## Source C

Soviet painting from 1937, by Fedot Vasilyevich Sychkov, showing peasants selling produce at a market. The image was produced as part of a government campaign.

## Exam-style question, Section B

How useful are Sources A and B for an enquiry into the living standards of citizens of the Soviet Union in the 1930s?

Explain your answer, using Sources A and B and your knowledge of the historical context.    **8 marks**

## Exam tip

First identify the impression you get from each source, then explain what they are useful for, and any limits to their use. Finally, compare the information in them to what else you know about the situation in the 1930s, to assess their accuracy or completeness.

## Summary

- Working and living conditions were often hard in the Soviet Union during the 1930s.
- In general, things were worse on collective farms than in towns and factories.
- Consumer goods were in short supply, but party and government members had better access to these than ordinary citizens.
- Female workers found that their pay and career opportunities lagged behind those of men.

## Checkpoint

### Strengthen

**S1** Write a 'Dear diary…' entry saying what life was like living in a town in the 1930s.

**S2** Write another 'Dear diary…' entry saying what life was like living on a collective farm in the 1930s.

### Challenge

**C1** Why were party and government members allowed greater access to consumer goods?

**C2** What made life harder on collective farms than in the towns and cities?

How confident are you about your answers to these questions? Ask your teacher to read them and suggest areas where you could improve them.

## Women in the Soviet Union

In 1930, the *Zhenotdel* – the women's section of the Communist Party (see page 70) – was closed down. Its job had been to promote improved conditions for women and equality with men. The Communist Party and the government were overwhelmingly male – and there was little enthusiasm for women's rights. Many male communists felt that the *Zhenotdel* was no longer needed.

## The official view of family life

Under Stalin, there was an end to experimentation in family life – which had included easy access to divorce and abortion.

The state now supported:

### *Marriage*

Stalin's view was that men and women should marry, and stay married. The breakdown of marriages had led to gangs of abandoned children roaming the streets in some cities – causing trouble and committing crimes. The ease of getting divorces, encouraged some men to abandon their families and give up supporting their children.

After 1936, it became more difficult to get a divorce – expensive fees were introduced that most workers could not afford. Men who left their families were fined if they didn't provide financial support. To discourage unmarried women from getting pregnant, paternity suits* were banned.

### Key term

**Paternity suit***

A legal action in which an unmarried mother sues the father of her child for financial support.

### Source A

A 1940s poster showing a conventional Soviet family of mother, father and child. The caption reads, 'To a beloved family, to peaceful work!'

К ЛЮБИМОЙ СЕМЬЕ,
К МИРНОМУ ТРУДУ!

### *A growing population*

Stalin wanted to encourage growth in the Soviet population – to provide workers for the new factories built in the Five-Year Plans. In 1936 abortions (made legal in 1920) were banned. This was very hard to

## Key term

**Sterilisation***

An operation to prevent a man or a woman from having children.

enforce, and many women – struggling to both work and raise families in cramped accommodation – resorted to unsafe, secret abortions, by people with no medical qualifications. Women were often left damaged by these illegal procedures. Infant mortality went up between 1935 and 1940, and this may have been due to these illegal abortions being counted as infant deaths. At the same time, it became harder to find contraceptives, and sterilisation* became illegal. To encourage families to have lots of children, the state gave women a financial allowance for their 7th child (and any further children!) up until their 3rd birthday.

### Heterosexual relationships

In 1933, a new law, Article 121, was added to the criminal code of the Soviet Union. It made male homosexuality illegal – with up to five years of hard labour in prison for men convicted. It made no mention of women.

## Source B

From an official government statement, issued in 1935.

The state cannot exist without the family. Marriage has a positive value for the Soviet Socialist state only if partners see in it a lifelong union.

## Interpretation 1

From *A History of the Soviet Union, 1917–1991*, by G. Hosking, published in 1992.

The breakup of families [in the late 1920s] meant a huge increase in the number of orphans. Many simply roamed the streets and begged. Others formed into gangs who would attack and rob people in the street or even invade and ransack apartment blocks.

## Activities

1  With a partner, discuss Source A. What can you infer about the official view of Soviet family life by the 1930s?

2  Interpretation 1 is about crime. What is the connection between this information and the way official attitudes towards family and marriage changed in the mid-1930s?

3  Do you think the women in Source C would have approved of the way official attitudes were changing? Think about things they might have approved or disapproved of – and why.

## Source C

Women workers commenting on the new law to ban abortion, in 1936. These views were collected by female Communist Party researchers investigating women's lives in the 1930s. They were largely ignored by male Communist Party members at the time, but were later published by the historian S. Fitzpatrick, in 1999.

Woman 1: My family lives with another family in a room of 30 metres. Have I the right to allow myself the luxury of bringing a second child into this environment? I think not.

Woman 2: I live with three children in a 12-metre room. And however great my desire to have a fourth child, I cannot allow myself to do so.

**Cause and consequence (2b)**

### Events and conditions

Study the living graph below, which is an assessment of the relative importance of the causes leading to collectivisation.

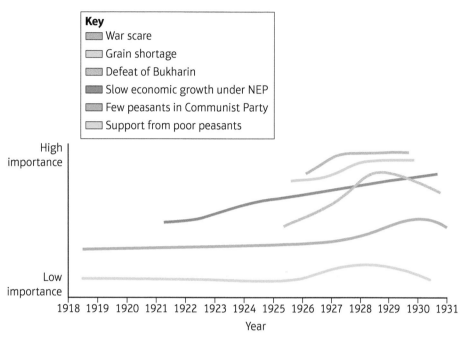

Make your own living graph to show why Stalin ended experimentation in family life in the 1930s, using the following causes. The years should run from 1919–1936.

| In the 1930s, the primary role of women was still seen as caring for the family rather than working. | Male party leaders were not interested in changing the situation of women. | During the First Five-Year Plan (1928–32) abortions went up as women tried to limit family size. |
|---|---|---|
| Increased industrialisation in the USSR, after 1928, required a larger workforce. | From the mid-1920s, quick and easy divorces left many children without financial support from their fathers. | Family breakdown, between 1917 and 1936, increased the numbers of orphans, along with street crime. |

1 Which of the causes would you describe as '**conditions**' and which would you describe as '**triggers**'? Explain your answer. Are there any that don't fit either term?

2 Which of the causes would you describe as 'long-term' and which would you describe as 'short-term'?

3 How does knowing the different levels of importance that the causes had, at different times, help you to explain why an event happened?

## Changes in employment

In the 1930s more women were working than ever before. In 1928, about three million women were at work – by 1940, this had leapt up to 13 million. In 1937, women made up 40% of all industrial workers, and 82% of all newly-hired workers.

Even so, most of these jobs were in industries that had traditionally employed female workers – such as textile manufacturing. Posters and films might show female welders, engineers and diggers of the Moscow Metro tunnels – but these stood out because they were *not* typical. In most of these heavy industries the workers were men.

Women had an increased economic role – but not an improved position in society. The Soviet Union was a very male-run society; and women were still expected to look after the home, even though more of them were going out to work during the Five-Year Plans. This was typical of most countries around the world in the 1930s – but the communists had once promised something very different.

## Source D

An official 1930s poster promoting International Labour Day with an image of women working in a factory.

## Interpretation 2

From *Women's Studies Encyclopedia, Volume 3*, by H. Tierney, published in 1999.

*The industrialisation of the Soviet Union benefitted women by drawing them into the workforce in huge numbers, but it did little to lighten their burden.*

*They continued to shoulder the burden of domestic work in addition to work outside the home...*

*Burdened by domestic responsibilities, child care, and work outside the home, most Soviet women were hampered in their efforts for self-improvement by a simple lack of time for education and professional growth.*

## The political position of women

Officially, the Soviet Union had gender-equality. However, women rarely held management jobs and, overall, female pay was well below that of male workers. There were also few women in leading positions in the Communist Party. By 1930, only 13.5% of party members were women. This makes Stalin's decision to close down the *Zhenotdel* that year – because women's problems had been 'solved' – rather shocking. It shows how unimportant its work was to many leading Communist Party members – despite the claims made about women's rights.

## Interpretation 3

From *Political and Economic Encyclopaedia of the Soviet Union and Eastern Europe*, by S. White, published in 1990.

*The numerous problems faced by women such as queues for food, lack of contraceptives, an inhumane abortion system and chauvinist [anti-female] male attitudes at work and at home were not discussed openly so long as ideologists loudly proclaimed that the 'Woman Question' had been solved. Not until 50 years after the Russian Revolution was the 'Woman Question' proclaimed 'unsolved'.*

### Exam-style question, Section B

Suggest **one** reason why Interpretations 2 and 3 give different views about what prevented women's lives from improving in the 1930s.

You may use Sources C and D to help explain your answer. **4 marks**

### Exam tip

Identify any differences you can find between the interpretations' views of what prevented women's rights from improving. Then decide why the differences in interpretations might have occurred. You can use Sources C and D to help – do they support different explanations?

## Key terms

**Ethnic minority***

Group with a different religion, language or traditions to the majority of the local population.

**Self-determination***

The right of a group of people to govern themselves.

# Ethnic minorities in the Soviet Union

Like women, ethnic minorities* found that there was a difference between the promises of equality and liberation in official propaganda, and their real-life everyday experiences. For example, promotions for Jews and Asians, during the Five-Year Plans, fell behind those for Russians, in the same way that opportunities for women were behind those experienced by men.

## The official communist view of nationalities in the Soviet Union

In November 1917, the Bolsheviks issued the *Declaration of the Rights of the Peoples of Russia*. In this they promised the different peoples of the tsarist empire:

- equality
- self-determination* – even including the right to leave and be independent
- freedom of religion (especially important as in central Asia, and elsewhere in the Soviet Union, many people were Muslim)
- the right to develop their own culture and lifestyle.

The hope was that, eventually, national differences would fade away; but they proved to be longer-lasting than communism in the Soviet Union.

In 1913, Stalin had written a book entitled *Marxism and the National Question*. Because he was a Georgian – not a Russian – he was soon considered something of an expert on minority ethnic groups in Russia. In fact, he was happy to see Russia dominate the other national groups.

## Source E

A 1937 poster showing Stalin and children from different ethnic groups in the Soviet Union.

## The ethnic makeup of the Soviet Union

When the Soviet Union was established in 1922, after the Civil War, it was described as a 'federation of nationalities'. This meant that it was made up of different self-governing national groups that, together, formed one country. The very first census of the Soviet Union was held in 1926, and it listed 172 distinct nationalities. Only 55% of the population of the Soviet Union was Russian – so how to keep this complex country together was an important issue.

There were 15 large nations (see Figure 4.6), each organised as a Soviet Socialist Republic or SSR. All of these SSRs were regarded as being equals. All of them also had significant ethnic minority populations within them.

There were other ethnic groups that did not have their own self-governing region – including Bulgarians, Greeks, Gypsies, Hungarians, Koreans, Poles and Volga Germans*.

## Key term

**Volga Germans***

People of German origin who lived along the Volga River.

**Figure 4.6** The republics of the Soviet Union by 1941.

# Persecution of ethnic minorities

In the 1930s, promotion of non-Russian languages and culture – which had once been communist policy – became considered a sign of disloyalty to the Soviet Union. During the Great Terror, leaders, teachers, writers and artists from national minorities were rounded up. There were even quotas for how many members of ethnic minorities should be arrested.

In the mid-1930s, many groups were forcibly moved away from border areas. For example, in 1937, over 171,000 Koreans were deported from the border regions of the Russian Far East to central Asia. They ended up in Kazakhstan and Uzbekistan. Many of their descendants are still there.

When the Soviet Union invaded eastern Poland in September 1939 – as part of a deal with Nazi Germany – about a million Poles were arrested and sent to the Gulag. In 1940 – as the Soviet Union seized control of Estonia, Latvia and Lithuania – about 56,000 (mostly middle-class) people were arrested and sent to labour camps. In 1941, when Germany invaded the Soviet Union, the Volga Germans – who had lived in Russia since the 18th century – were arrested and exiled to Siberia and Central Asia, where huge numbers died. At the same time, about 89,000 Finns were deported to Kazakhstan.

### Why was the communist government suspicious of these minorities?

People from ethnic groups that also lived in countries across the borders of the Soviet Union were distrusted. The communist government was particularly worried about the loyalty of Finns and Poles living in the Soviet Union – as Finland and Poland shared borders with the Soviet Union.

Minorities living deep within the Soviet Union were distrusted too. It was feared they would become too independent of the government in Moscow. They were denounced as 'Bourgeois Nationalists'.

## Extend your knowledge

**Murdered Polish prisoners**

During the invasion of Poland, in 1939, the Soviet Union deported officers of the defeated Polish army to Russia. They were joined there by well-educated Poles who had been arrested by Stalin's secret police – including university lecturers, lawyers and doctors. In 1940, the secret police murdered these 22,000 prisoners and buried them in mass graves in Katyn Forest, near the city of Smolensk. The aim was to remove the leadership of the Polish nation.

## Activities

1 Look at Source E. What can you infer about the official view of ethnic minorities in the Soviet Union?

2 With a partner discuss Source E. Was life in the Soviet Union really favourable to ethnic minorities? Think about the way the Soviet Union was structured and changed over time.

## Summary

- In the middle of the 1930s, Stalin made it more difficult to divorce, get contraceptives, and have an abortion – it was a return to pre-Revolutionary family values.
- Women had more job opportunities – but not real equality with men.
- Ethnic minorities found that – despite the official promises made to them – their rights and cultures came increasingly under pressure from the mid-1930s onwards.

## Checkpoint

### Strengthen

**S1** Under the titles: Marriage, Population and Heterosexual relationships – make notes on how attitudes to family life changed in the mid-1930s.

**S2** Create a timeline showing how treatment of ethnic minorities changed in the Soviet Union in this period.

### Challenge

**C1** Why was Stalin distrustful of Finns, Germans, Koreans and Poles? Give examples of how they were treated.

**C2** Imagine you are Stalin: explain what you mean when you accuse some people of being 'Bourgeois Nationalists' – and why you are determined to crush them.

How confident do you feel about your answers? You could look up the minorities mentioned above online, and see how the information you find adds to your answer.

# Recap: Economic and social changes, 1924–41

## Recall quiz

1  What is the Russian word for 'harmony' that was used to describe the relationship between workers and peasants under the NEP?

2  What year was the 'war scare'?

3  What was the 'Urals-Siberian method'?

4  What is the Russian word for a collective farm?

5  Which republic of the Soviet Union suffered most in the collectivisation famine?

6  What was the Russian name of the State Planning Committee?

7  Name the miner who was said to have dug 14 times his daily quota of coal.

8  What did Stalin's government introduce in 1932, to try to control the movement of people around the Soviet Union?

9  In what year was abortion made illegal?

10  What percentage of the industrial workforce of the Soviet Union was female by 1937?

## Activity ?

### Turning points

Historians often use the phrase 'turning point' to describe an important event that changes the course of history. Look back over what you have learned in this book about how Russia (and then the Soviet Union) changed between 1917 and 1941.

Choose three 'turning points' that you think were more important than other events in deciding the course of Russian history. For each turning point explain:

• what happened

• why it was important

• why you have selected it as a 'turning point'.

After you have done this, compare your three 'turning points' with those of a neighbour. How similar/different were your decisions?

Now decide which of your three turning points is most important. Write it on a sticky note. As a class take turns to stick your notes on the board, grouping similar notes together. Does one turning point get most votes? As a class, discuss why.

## Activity ?

### Lenin or Stalin?

Both Lenin and Stalin were revolutionaries who aimed to change their country dramatically. Which would you choose as the most important revolutionary of the two? Prepare a short speech to give to the class. When everyone has spoken, take a class vote.

Finally write a short essay, explaining the reasons for your choice more fully. Include:

• the situation they faced

• the things they did and changed

• their successes and failures

• a conclusion summarising the reasons for your choice.

# Explaining why historians' interpretations differ

In Paper 3, one question will ask you to suggest one reason why two interpretations give different views about an aspect of your study. To understand the reasons for difference you need to appreciate that historians writing about any society have to make choices and they have to make judgements. They choose what to concentrate on. They also come to views about the topics they research. Historians may be focusing on different aspects, using different sources, or reaching different conclusions on the same sources. These factors explain reasons for difference.

## Historians focus on different things

Interpretations of history are created by historians. Historians construct interpretations based on evidence from the past. Think of their role as similar to a house-builder: the evidence, that is the sources available, provides the building blocks for their construction. Historians choose what enquiries to make of the materials available to them. No historian can write about the whole of history everywhere. What shapes the historian's work is what they want to explore and what they choose to focus on. Figure 1 below lists some of the choices they make.

| Place | National history | Local history |
|---|---|---|
| Period | One century or more | One decade or less |
| Range | Overview | Depth |
| People | National leaders | Ordinary people |
| Aspect | Political history | Social history |

**Figure 1** Some examples of historians' choices.

**Figure 2** The historian's focus.

After choosing their focus, the historian must find evidence to pursue their enquiry. So, they will be looking for different things in order to answer different questions about the past.

Historians A and B below are both writing about the same school, but their focus is different. In looking at the history of a school, several different enquiries are possible: for example, the focus could be on the building, the curriculum, students' achievements – and so on. As you read the interpretations below, identify what the two historians are interested in. What have their enquiries focused on?

### Historian A

The village school has been in continuous use since 1870. It continues to educate local children from the ages of 5–11. They are educated in the same building that was constructed in 1870. Its outward appearance has hardly changed. It was originally built of red brick, with white-painted wooden doors, and the large windows that can still be seen today. The schoolroom windows, reaching almost to the high ceiling, were designed to give plenty of light, but with windowsills too high for students to be distracted by being able to see anything outside. Although a modern extension at the rear was added in the 1960s, the key features of the school building represent a remarkable degree of continuity in education in the locality.

### Historian B

Education locally has changed in the period since 1870. Lessons in the 19th century focused almost entirely on the 3Rs of reading, writing and arithmetic. There was much learning by heart and copying out of passages. By the 21st century, the wall displays, and the students' exercise books, show that science, history, geography, have all become important parts of the curriculum, and with more emphasis on finding out and creativity. In terms of the curriculum, the degree of change in education since 1870 has been considerable.

Read each of the statements about Historians A and B below.

**a** The historians have different views about the amount of change in education in the village.

**b** One of the historians is wrong.

**c** One of the historians is biased.

**d** They are just giving different opinions.

**e** They have used different evidence.

**f** They have focused on different aspects.

**g** They are both correct in their conclusions.

**h** They have emphasised different things.

**i** They are looking for different things.

**j** The historians disagree.

**k** The historians do not disagree.

**1** Make two lists: one of statements you agree with and another of those you disagree with.

**2** Explain why Historians A and B have different views about the extent to which education has changed in the village. Try to use words from the box below in your answer:

| focus | emphasis | aspect | evidence | conclusions | enquiry | interested |
|---|---|---|---|---|---|---|

## Historians reach different conclusions from the evidence

Even when historians have the same focus and purpose – for example, they are both seeking to explain why the same thing happened – their conclusions may still be different. This is because evidence from the past doesn't provide us with an answer: historians have to work out an answer from it, and often the evidence points in different directions. When this happens, historians have to make judgements. Differences may arise because:

- they have given weight to different sources or
- they have reached different conclusions on the same sources.

In a court of law, every member of the jury hears the same evidence, but they sometimes disagree about their verdict. It comes down to making judgements about what conclusions can be drawn from the evidence.

Study Interpretations 1 and 2 on page 85.

**1** Which of the following reasons explains why the views in Interpretations 1 and 2 are different? Make a list of all those that you think apply. You can add other reasons of your own if you wish.

**a** The historians are interested in different aspects of the topic.

**b** The historians have emphasised different things when giving their views.

**c** The evidence from the period points in different directions.

**d** The historians have reached conclusions by giving weight to different sources from the period.

**2** Choose one reason you have listed, and write one or two sentences to explain why you chose it. Remember to use the interpretations in your answer. Refer to sources from the period too, if you listed reason c or d.

- A historian's work is shaped by the aspect of history they choose to explore.
- Historians' judgements differ because evidence can support different views. They may reach different conclusions because they have given weight to different sources or because they are looking at different aspects of the topic.

# Preparing for your GCSE Paper 3 exam

## Paper 3 overview

Your Paper 3 is in two sections that examine the Modern Depth Study. In Section A you answer one question on a source and one using your own knowledge. Section B is a case study using sources and interpretations of history, and the four questions will be about the same issue. The paper is worth 30% of your History assessment.

| Section | History Paper 3: Modern Depth Study | | Time |
|---|---|---|---|
| A | Answer 2 questions | 16 marks | 20 minutes |
| B | Answer 4 questions | 32 marks + 4 for SPaG | 60 minutes |

## Modern Depth Option 30: Russia and the Soviet Union, 1917–41

## Section A

You will answer Questions 1 and 2.

### Q1 Give two things you can infer from Source A about… (4 marks)

Source A is on the question paper. You should work out two inferences from it. An inference is something not directly stated in the source, but which you can support using details from it.

You have a table to complete for each inference: 'What I can infer …' and 'Details in the source that tell me this'. Allow five minutes to read the source and to write your answer. This question is only worth four marks and you should keep the answer brief and not try to put more information on extra lines.

### Q2 Explain why… (12 marks)

This question asks you to explain the reasons why something happened. Allow 15 minutes to write your answer. You are given two information points as prompts to help you. You do not have to use the prompts and you will not lose marks by leaving them out. Always remember to add in a new point of your own as well: higher marks are gained by adding in a point extra to the prompts.

You will be given at least two pages of lines in the answer booklet for your answer. This does not mean you should try to fill all the space. The front page of the exam paper tells you 'there may be more space than you need'. Aim to write an answer giving at least three explained reasons.

## Section B

You will answer Question 3 (a), (b), (c) and (d). All four questions will be about the same issue. Question (a) will be based on contemporary sources (evidence from the period you are studying). Questions (b) (c) and (d) will be based on two historical interpretations.

### Q3(a) How useful are Sources A and B for an enquiry into… (8 marks)

You are given two sources to evaluate. They are in a separate sources booklet so you can keep them in front of you while you write your answer. Allow 15 minutes for this question to give yourself time to read both sources carefully. Make sure your answer deals with both sources and use your knowledge when you evaluate the source. You could use it, for example, to evaluate the accuracy or completeness of the evidence. You should make a judgement about the usefulness of each source, giving clear reasons. Only choose points that are directly relevant to the enquiry in the question. You should always take account of the provenance (the nature, origin and purpose) of the source when you think about the usefulness of the information it gives. How reliable is it?

### Q3(b) Study Interpretations 1 and 2. They give different views about…

### What is the main difference between these views? (4 marks)

Allow ten minutes for this question, to give yourself time to read the interpretations. Identify an overall difference rather than different pieces of information. For example, think about whether one is positive and the other negative. Then use details from both interpretations. The difference is… this is shown because Interpretation 1 says… but Interpretation 2 says…

*Q3(c) Suggest one reason why Interpretations 1 and 2 give different views about...*

Allow five minutes for this question. It does not need a long answer (it is only worth four marks) and you have already read the interpretations; but you will need to use both the interpretations again and perhaps Sources B and C. Give a clear reason for the difference. One reason could be that the historians have chosen to give weight to different evidence. If you use this reason, you should use Sources B and C to show how the evidence from the period differs. If you give a different reason for the difference, for example you think the historians have a different focus (see pages 142–43), you will not need to use Sources B and C.

*Q3(d) How far do you agree with Interpretation [1 or 2] about... ? (16 marks + 4 marks SPaG)*

This question, including SPaG, is worth 20 marks – over one third of your marks for the whole of the Modern Depth Study. Make sure you have kept 30 minutes of the exam time to answer it and to check your spelling, punctuation and grammar. You will already have worked out the views in the two interpretations for Question (b). Question (d) asks you how far you agree with the view in one of them. Plan your answer before you begin to write, and put your points in two columns: For and Against.

You should use points from the two interpretations and also use your own contextual knowledge. Think of it as putting weight on each side of the argument, as you decide what your judgement is going to be for the conclusion. That way your whole answer will hang together – it will be coherent. Be clear about your reasons (your criteria) for your judgement.

In this question, four extra marks will be given for good spelling, punctuation and grammar. Use sentences, paragraphs, capital letters, commas and full stops. Try also to use relevant specialist terms – for example, terms such as constitution, communism or legislation.

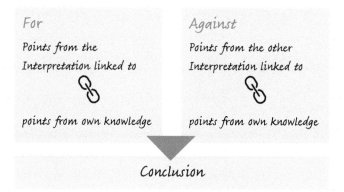

For
Points from the Interpretation linked to
points from own knowledge

Against
Points from the other Interpretation linked to
points from own knowledge

Conclusion

# Paper 3, Section A: Question 1

Study Source H on page 126.
Give **two** things you can infer from Source H about achievements in Soviet industry in 1930. **(4 marks)**

Study Source H on page 126.

## Exam tip

Make two inferences and choose details from the source that directly support them. The examples below give only the first inference and support.

### Average answer

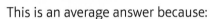

What I can infer:
*Setting up factories like the one in Stalingrad was quite impressive.*
Details in the source that tell me this:
*It was very big and building it had made history.*

> The answer identifies something about why such factories were important but the details do not come from the source.

### Verdict

This is an average answer because:
- It lacks definite and specific inference as to why such a factory was important to industry and it is not supported by precise detail from the source.

Use the feedback to rewrite this answer, making as many improvements as you can.

**5th**

### Strong answer

What I can infer:
*The source suggests that Soviet industry was transformed by huge and rapid expansion in the 1930s.*
Details in the source that tell me this:
*It only took two years for the first tractor works to go from a building site to working at full capacity. At the time of writing Soviet industry produces the largest number of tractors in the world.*

> Details are given that support a correct inference.

### Verdict

This is a strong answer because:
- The information from the source supports both the speed and extent of industrial expansion.

**7th**

# Paper 3, Section A: Question 2

Explain why Stalin wanted to industrialise the USSR so rapidly. You may use the following in your answer:

- foreign threats
- the Communist Party

You **must** also use information of your own. **(12 marks)**

### Exam tip

Focus on explaining 'why'. Aim to give at least three clear reasons.

## Average answer

Stalin wanted to industrialise the USSR quickly because he was afraid that the USSR might be attacked by foreign enemies. Many other countries did not like communism and in 1927 there was concern in the USSR that a war might soon break out and Stalin was worried that if it did then the USSR would be defeated. To avoid this, he decided to launch the Five-Year Plans. In 1928 the First Five-Year Plan started.

Stalin also wanted to get more workers who would support the Communist Party. The communists looked to the workers for their greatest amount of support as these were the people who benefitted most from communist rule and the communists claimed to have seized power on their behalf in October 1917.

As well as these reasons, Stalin also wanted to take away support from people like Trotsky, Zinoviev and Kamenev who he had just defeated in the Power Struggle and whose supporters could still be found in the Communist Party even after Stalin won the Power Struggle.

The information here is accurate but too descriptive. There is some development of the significance of the war scare, but most of it is not directly linked to an explanation of why this led to rapid industrialisation.

Relevant information is given here and explains how the Communist Party looked to the working class for its main support. However, it needs to be directly linked to the question that is asked.

An additional reason for rapid industrialisation is given, but is not fully developed. It should also refer to why this encouraged rapid industrialisation and what Stalin expected to gain from this.

## Verdict

This is an average answer because:

- The answer information is accurate, showing some knowledge and understanding of the period, and adds a point additional to the stimulus (so it is not a weak answer).
- It does not analyse causes explicitly enough to be a strong answer.
- There is some development of material but not enough of a connection made between this material and the question being asked.

Use the feedback to rewrite this answer, making as many improvements as you can.

# Paper 3, Section A: Question 2

Explain why Stalin wanted to industrialise the USSR so rapidly. You may use the following in your answer:
- foreign threats
- the Communist Party.

You **must** also use information of your own. **(12 marks)**

## Strong answer

Stalin knew how backward the USSR was when compared to other countries. In 1927 there was fear of war breaking out and Stalin wanted to ensure that communism would not fall, in the way that the tsar and Kerensky had because they could not cope with problems caused by war. By launching the Five-Year Plan in 1928, Stalin hoped to turn the USSR into a modern industrial country that was capable of manufacturing weapons to defend itself.

> The information here is accurate and develops a line of reasoning which links this factor to Stalin's decision to industrialise rapidly after 1927.

Stalin also wanted to industrialise rapidly because this greatly increased the numbers of workers and extended the power base of the Communist Party. In 1928 there were only 4.6 million workers in the USSR; but by 1940 this had risen to 12.6 million. They were grateful to the party for new jobs (unemployment vanished). Stakhanovites were particularly loyal to the communist regime and there was real enthusiasm among young people for the 'adventure' of modernising the USSR.

> Accurate and relevant information is given here and, by addressing the question directly, it is used to explain how industrialisation strengthened the party.

As well as these reasons, Stalin also wanted to take away support from his previous rivals for power. People like Trotsky, Zinoviev and Kamenev, who he had defeated in the Power Struggle and whose supporters could still be found. They had argued for rapid industrialisation and by taking on this task Stalin encouraged those who had once supported them now to throw their support behind him.

> An additional reason for rapid industrialisation is given and it explains what Stalin expected to gain from this. This shows wide ranging knowledge.

## Verdict

This is a strong answer because:
- The well-chosen information is accurate, showing good knowledge and understanding of the period, and adds a point additional to the stimulus.
- It analyses causes explicitly and the argument is well structured and logical.
- There is a clear connection made between all of this and the question being answered.

# Paper 3, Section B: Question 3a

Study Sources B and C on page 20. How useful are Sources B and C for an enquiry into the causes of the February Revolution in 1917? Explain your answer, using Sources B and C and your knowledge of the historical context. **(8 marks)**

### Exam tip

Consider the strengths and weaknesses of the evidence. Your evaluation must link to the enquiry and use contextual knowledge. Your reasons (criteria) for judgement should be clear. Include points about:

- what information is relevant and what you can infer from the source
- how the provenance (nature, origin, purpose) of each source affects its usefulness.

## Average answer

Source B is useful because it shows that soldiers were involved in the disturbances that were a key part of the February Revolution. Everyone in the photograph is in military uniform and they appear to be happy to pose for the picture, which suggests they were proud of their actions. The numbers of people shown reveal that a lot of soldiers must have been part of such protests.

> Comments show that information can be got from the photograph. Knowledge is added to show that the photograph is probably reliable. It would be stronger with more developed evaluation.

Source C is useful because it shows that mass and unplanned unrest led to the February Revolution, which suggests that things got out of hand without anyone actually planning this beforehand.

> Some useful information is taken from the source. The answer begins an inference ('which suggests that…') but this needs to be more developed and better supported.

It is also useful because it was produced by the tsar's secret police who spied on the enemies of the tsar and put together detailed reports on what was going on in Russia. On the other hand, it only tells it from the tsar's side so this limits how much we can use what it says about what led up to the events of the February Revolution in 1917.

> Comments are made about the authorship and purpose of the source, but they assume that because it comes from one side in the conflict it must be unreliable. Additional knowledge is used to explain what such a report might show and this should be made clearer.

## Verdict

This is an average answer because:

- It has taken relevant information from both sources and shown some analysis by beginning to make an inference (so it is not a weak answer).
- It has added relevant knowledge drawn from an idea about the wider context and has used it for some evaluation of both the sources, but this is not sufficiently developed.
- It does not explain the criteria for judgement clearly enough to be a strong answer. The evaluation of the provenance of the sources should be more developed.

Use the feedback to rewrite this answer, making as many improvements as you can.

# Paper 3, Section B: Question 3a

Study Sources B and C on page 20.

How useful are Sources B and C for an enquiry into the causes of the February Revolution in 1917?

Explain your answer, using Sources B and C and your knowledge of the historical context. **(8 marks)**

## Strong answer

Source B is useful because it gives direct evidence that large numbers of soldiers were involved in the disturbances in February 1917. The fact that they are openly posing for the photograph indicates that the authorities must have lost control over large numbers of their troops. On the other hand, it is only one photograph and may have been taken because a picture of revolutionary soldiers looked particularly dramatic. It may give a misleading impression of the importance of soldiers in the February Revolution, especially as other evidence indicates that civilians (including many women) played a major part in challenging the tsar.

> Strengths and limitations of the source are shown and contextual knowledge is used in the evaluation, which also comments on the nature of the source.

Source C is even more useful because it gives a broader view of events and looks at the role of civilian protesters as well as rebellious soldiers. This gives us a more balanced idea of the events and is very useful as we can use this to show that the February Revolution was not planned but arose out of actions that got out of control. This is in line with other evidence which shows that uncoordinated protests combined with military mutinies.

> Good analysis of the source evidence and integration of own knowledge.

Its usefulness is increased because it is from the tsar's secret police and would have been a secret report, not produced for publication. This means that the impression it gives of a series of spontaneous protests, that got out of hand when soldiers refused to crush them, is probably an accurate picture of what happened during the confused days of February 1917. This is consistent with the fact that revolutionary groups were taken by surprise and played no part in planning the February Revolution.

> Good evaluation, taking authorship, nature and purpose of the source into account. In addition, there is good knowledge of the historical context – which is used to assess the usefulness of the information provided in this source.

## Verdict

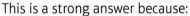

This is a strong answer because:

- It has analysed both sources critically and assessed them.
- It has used contextual knowledge in the evaluation of both of the sources.
- The evaluation takes authorship, nature and purpose of the sources into account and explains this clearly when making judgements about their usefulness.

# Paper 3, Section B: Questions 3b & 3c

Study Interpretations 1 and 2 on pages 21 and 22. They give different views about the causes of the February Revolution in 1917.
What is the main difference between these views?
Explain your answer, using details from both interpretations. **(4 marks)**

### Average answer

*A main difference is that Interpretation 1 emphasises that it was the fault of Tsar Nicholas, who made a mistake. Interpretation 2 emphasises the mixture of events that led to the revolution, ranging from losses in the war to food shortages and high prices.*

A valid difference is identified but no details are given from Interpretation 1.

### Verdict

This is an average answer because it identifies a difference, with some detail from Interpretation 2, but it does not use detail from Interpretation 1 to support the difference.
Use the feedback to rewrite this answer, making as many improvements as you can.

Suggest **one** reason why Interpretations 1 and 2 give different views about the causes of the February Revolution in 1917.
You may use Sources B and C to help explain your answer. **(4 marks)**

### Average answer

*The interpretations may differ because the historians have emphasised different sources of evidence. For example, Source B suggests that losing control of soldiers was important. That supports Interpretation 1, which emphasises that it was ordering soldiers in to break up the protests that led to a crisis that got out of control.*

A reason is given and Source B is used, but nothing is said about Interpretation 2 or Source C.

### Verdict

This is an average answer because it gives a reason for the different views with support from Source B, but Source C has not been used.
Use the feedback to rewrite this answer, making as many improvements as you can.

# Paper 3, Section B: Questions 3b & 3c

Study Interpretations 1 and 2 on pages 21 and 22. They give different views about the causes of the February Revolution in 1917.

What is the main difference between these views?

Explain your answer, using details from both interpretations. **(4 marks)**

### Strong answer

*A main difference is that Interpretation 1 emphasises the role of the tsar in causing the protests to spiral out of control by ordering in troops to crush the protests. Interpretation 2 emphasises the mixture of events that led to the revolution, ranging from losses in the war to food shortages and high prices.*

Details from Interpretation 1 are used, as well as from Interpretation 2.

### Verdict

This is a strong answer because it identifies a valid difference with support from both interpretations.

Suggest **one** reason why Interpretations 1 and 2 give different views about the causes of the February Revolution in 1917.

You may use Sources B and C to help explain your answer. **(4 marks)**

### Strong answer

*The interpretations may differ because the historians have emphasised different sources of evidence. For example, Source B suggests that the authorities had lost control of soldiers. That supports Interpretation 1, which emphasises that it was ordering soldiers in to break up the protests that led to a crisis that got out of control.*

*Source C provides some support for Interpretation 2, which stresses the food shortages and high prices that led to the protests. Source C mentions the supply crisis (meaning lack of food) which triggered the street protests.*

Details from Source C are used to show support for Interpretation 2 as well as details from Source B to support Interpretation 1.

### Verdict

This is a strong answer because it gives a valid reason for the different views and supports it using both sources.

# Paper 3, Section B: Question 3d

**Up to four marks of the total for part (d) will be awarded for spelling, punctuation, grammar and use of specialist terminology.**

How far do you agree with Interpretation 1 about the reasons why the February Revolution against the rule of the tsar took place?

Explain your answer, using both interpretations and your knowledge of the historical context. **(20 marks)**

## Exam tip

Be clear what view the author gives and then consider points for and against this view from both interpretations and your own knowledge. Make a judgement, giving reasons for your decision.

SPaG is also assessed. Take care with spelling, punctuation and the use of sentences, paragraphs and historical terms.

## Average answer

Interpretation 1 says that what had started as just a riot over lack of food turned into something far more serious because the tsar sent a telegram ordering the use of soldiers to stop the protests. From my own knowledge I know that soldiers in Petrograd refused to obey their orders to fire on the crowds and these mutineers joined the protesters.

Relevant details are chosen from Interpretation 1 and own knowledge is included. But the knowledge is simply added on to the interpretation. The answer should explain clearly whether the information supports or challenges the view that is found in Interpretation 1.

But Interpretation 2 does not support this view that it was just the fault of the one telegram that the February revolt against tsarist rule occurred. It says that grievances were building up and this meant that when soldiers did not act against protesters it all exploded into revolution. I know that people by February 1917 were angry about the casualties in the war the way the war was being run low wages and the failure of the tsar to solve these problems as well as the food shortages. So I do not agree with Interpretation 1. I agree with Interpretation 2 that it was these longer-term reasons that really led to the February Revolution.

Relevant details are chosen to contrast Interpretation 1 with Interpretation 2 and own knowledge is added in. A judgement is given, but this is not well explained.

## Verdict

This is an average answer because:

- It has chosen relevant details from both the interpretations and used contextual knowledge in the answer (so it is not a weak answer).
- It does not explain reasons for the judgement clearly enough to be a strong answer.
- Spelling is accurate and there is some use of specialist terms (mutineers), but this is not wide-ranging and punctuation is limited to the use of full stops.

Use the feedback to rewrite this answer, making as many improvements as you can.

# Paper 3, Section B: Question 3d

**Up to four marks of the total for part (d) will be awarded for spelling, punctuation, grammar and use of specialist terminology.**

How far do you agree with Interpretation 1 about the reasons why the February Revolution against the rule of the tsar took place?

Explain your answer, using both interpretations and your knowledge of the historical context. **(20 marks)**

## Strong answer

Interpretation 1's view is that it was the tsar's telegram that turned what was just a riot over food into a widespread revolt that could no longer be contained. Clearly, using troops in this way did cause things to explode out of control.

On the other hand, Interpretation 2 suggests that the situation in Petrograd was much more serious than this, even before the tsar's order to use troops against the rioters arrived. It talks about widespread bitter and hostile discontent over a number of issues. The fact that the strikes and protests had been going on for days and growing in size would support this interpretation.

> The extracts are analysed to show contrasting views and contextual knowledge is integrated.

The views differ most about whether the situation was really dangerous before the telegram arrived from the tsar. Interpretation 1's view is that things were containable before this happened, while Interpretation 2 stresses the seriousness of the situation even before the telegram arrived. Given the way that the protests were growing in the month leading up to the tsar losing control, I think that Interpretation 2 makes a strong point in saying it was about more than one decision made by the tsar.

> A key issue is identified and there is good use of contextual knowledge to make a judgement.

It is possible to agree with both interpretations, since Interpretation 1 deals with a 'trigger event', which caused things to get out of control, and Interpretation 2 with the seriousness of what was building up before that, and that this was why the tsar's decision led to him losing control of Petrograd. It is clear that the telegram led to soldiers being used against protesters and that, when these soldiers mutinied, the protests moved up to a new level and soon turned into political revolution and not just economic complaints. This then caused the abdication of the tsar. Overall, Interpretation 2 is probably the best one as, while it also says that the actions of the soldiers were crucial, it helps us understand why this then turned so quickly to revolution against the rule of the tsar.

> A judgement is reached with clear reasons and both views are considered. Knowledge is very well used to support the judgement. Spelling, punctuation and grammar are good and appropriate specialist terminology is used (mutinied, political revolution, abdication).

## Verdict

This is a strong answer because:

- Both interpretations are analysed and evaluated using own knowledge.
- The reasoning is well explained and logical, and the judgement is appropriately justified with clear reasons given.
- SPaG demonstrates accuracy, effective control of meaning and the use of a wide range of specialist terms.

# Answers to recap quiz questions

## Chapter 1

1 Tsar Nicholas II
2 Socialist Revolutionaries (SRs)
3 Lenin
4 Duma
5 International Women's Day
6 The tsar was blamed for defeats
7 Soviet
8 The April Theses
9 General Kornilov
10 Trotsky

## Chapter 2

1 Constituent Assembly
2 Socialist Revolutionaries (SRs)
3 Treaty of Brest-Litovsk
4 Red
5 Trotsky
6 War Communism
7 Kronstadt
8 New Economic Policy
9 Zhenotdel
10 A way to get a divorce quickly and cheaply

## Chapter 3

1 Lenin's testament
2 Trotsky
3 Bukharin
4 Yezhov
5 Gulag
6 Slave labourers
7 Military/armed forces
8 Socialist Realism
9 1936
10 Cult of personality/Cult of Stalin

## Chapter 4

1 Smychka
2 1927
3 Taking grain from peasants by force
4 Kolkhoz
5 Ukraine
6 Gosplan
7 Stakhanov
8 Internal passports
9 1936
10 40%

# Index

# Acknowledgements

This book is dedicated to the history teachers and support staff at Kingdown School in Warminster: Russell, Tasha, Georgie, Sam, Ellie, Tom, Yvonne and Marianne. Their dedication to history and to the students in their care, and their humour and support, has made it a great experience being part of 'the History team'. Thank you.

## Picture Credits

The publisher would like to thank the following for their kind permission to reproduce their photographs:

(Key: b-bottom; c-centre; l-left; r-right; t-top)

**akg-images Ltd:** Archive Photos 92t, Universal Images Group / Sovfoto 97l, 97r; **Alamy Images:** Heritage Image Partnership Ltd 55, ITAR-TASS Photo Agency 133, Niday Picture Library 20; **Bridgeman Art Library Ltd:** Deutsches Historisches Museum, Berlin, Germany / © DHM 48, Lords Gallery, London, UK 6b, 59, Museum of the Revolution, Moscow, Russia 56, 66, Pictures from History 71, Pictures from History / Woodbury & Page 115, Private Collection 58, Private Collection / Photo © Tobie Mathew Collection 92b; **Getty Images:** David Pollack 125, Heritage Images 36, 76, 95tl, 95r, 95bl, 103, 104, 121, LAPI / Roger Viollet 138, Sovfoto UIG 10, 15, 35, 91, 110, 123, SVR2 117, Universal History Archive 6t; **Martyn Whittock:** 53; **Mary Evans Picture Library:** 60, Alexander Meledin 131, Sueddeutsche Zeitung Photo 114; **Rex Shutterstock:** Sovfoto / Universal Images Group 79, Universal History Archive / Universal Images Group 67, 136; **Shutterstock.com:** Daniel Korzeniewski 72, Vladislav Gurfinkel 42, 52; **TopFoto:** 8, 11, 29, HIP / Fine Art Images 132, The Granger Collection 32

**Cover images:** *Front:* **TopFoto:** Fine Art Images / Heritage Images

All other images © Pearson Education

**Picture Research by:** Jane Smith

*We are grateful to the following for permission to reproduce copyright material:*

## Text

Extract on page 15 in Interpretation 1 from *The Russian Revolution 1917–1932*, OUP (Fitzpatrick, S. 1982) p.33, by permission of Oxford University Press; Extract on page 19 in Source A from *Diary of M.M.Prishvin* (Prishvin, M.), Literary Heritage Publishers; Ryazanova Liliya Alexandrovna with permission; Extract on page 20 in Source C from *The Russian Revolution 1899–1919*, Fontana (Pipes, R. 1992) p.279, reprinted by permission of HarperCollins Publishers Ltd; © Richard Pipes 1992; Extract on page 21 in Interpretation 1 from *The Russian Revolution 1899–1919*, Fontana (Pipes. R 1992) p.276, reprinted by permission of HarperCollins Publishers Ltd; © Richard Pipes 1992; Extract on page 22 in Interpretation 2 from *Lenin, Hitler & Stalin*, Jonathan Cape (Gellately, R. 2007) p.22, The Random House group copyright © 2007 by Robert Gellately. Used by permission of Alfred A. and Knopf, an imprint of the Knopf Doubleday Publishing Group, a division of Penguin Random House LLC. All rights reserved; Extract on page 35 in Interpretation 2 from *Lenin: A Biography*, First ed., Macmillan (Service,R. 2000) p.313, reproduced with permission of Pan Macmillan via PLSclear; Extract on page 47 in Interpretation 1 from *The Soviet Union A Documentary Reader Vol 1, 1917–1940*, Exeter U.P (Acton, E. & Stableford, T. (eds) 2005) p.72, Liverpool University Press; Extract on page 47 in Interpretation 2 from *The Russian Rev. Lenin to Stalin, 1917–1929*, Papermac (Carr, E.H.), reproduced with permission of Palgrave Macmillan; Extract on page 56 in Source G from *The World Crisis: Volume IV: 1918–1928: The Aftermath* (Churchill, W.S.), reproduced with permission of Curtis Brown, London on behalf of The Estate of Winston S. Churchill. © The Estate of Winston S. Churchill; Extract on page 63 in Interpretation 1 from *The Russian Revolution from Lenin* to Stalin, 1917–1929, Palgrave Macmillan (Carr, E.H. 1979) p.35, reproduced with permission of Palgrave Macmillan; Extract on page 70 in Interpretation 1 from The Russian Revolution from Lenin to Stalin, 1917–1929, Palgrave Macmillan (1979), reproduced with permission of Palgrave Macmillan; Extract on page 85 in Interpretation 1 from Lenin. Life and Legacy, HarperCollins (Volkogonov, D. 1994) pp.483–4, reprinted by permission of HarperCollins Publishers Ltd, © (Volkogonov, D.) (1994); Extract on page 85 in Interpretation 2 from A People's Tragedy, Jonathan Cape (Figes, O. 1996) p.807, The Random House Group copyright © 1996 by Orlando Figes and used by permission of Viking Books, an imprint of Penguin Publishing Group, a division of Penguin Random House LLC; Extract on page 88 in Interpretation 3 from The Great Terror: A Reassessment, revised ed. Pimlico (Conquest, R. 1990) p.445, The Random House Group; Extract on page 91 in Source E,translation English and translation copyright © 1958 by William Collins Sons and Co. Ltd. Authorized and revisions to the English translation copyright © 1958 by Pantheon Books Inc. Copyright and renewed 1986 by Random House, Inc.. Used by permission of Pantheon Books, an imprint of the and Knopf Doubleday Publishing Group, a division of Penguin Random House LLC. All rights and reserved; Extract on page 99 in Interpretation 1 from Origins of the Great Purges: The Soviet Communist Party Reconsidered, 1933–1938, CUP (Getty, J.A. 1987) p.112; Extract on page 99 in Interpretation 2 from Stalinist Values: The Cultural Norms of Soviet Modernity, 1917–1941, Cornell University Press (Hoffman, D.L. 2003) p.150 reproduced with permission of Cornell University Press in the format Book via Copyright Clearance Center; Extract on page 101 in Interpretation 1 from A People's Tragedy, Jonathan Cape (Figes, O. 1996) p.822–3, The Random House Group copyright © 1996 by Orlando Figes. Used by permission of Viking Books, an imprint of Penguin Publishing Group, a division of Penguin Random House LLC; Extract on page 102 in Source A from Within the Whirlwind (Ginzburg, E.), reprinted by permission of HarperCollins Publishers Ltd and © Ginzburg, E; Extract on page 117 in Source E from http://www.holodomorct.org/, Connecticut Holodomor Committee, "Eyewitness Accounts" http://www.holodomorct.org/accounts.html; Extract on page 117 in Interpretation 1 from Socialist Planning, CUP (Ellman, M. 2014) p.196; Extract on page 121 in Interpretation 1 from An Economic History of the USSR, Penguin (Nove, A. 1989) p.148 & p.3, from An Economic History Of The USSR 1917–1991 by Alec Nove (Allen Lane The Penguin Press, 1969, Third edition, 1992) Copyright © Alec Nove, 1969, 1972, 1976, 1982, 1989, 1992; Extract on page 126 in Interpretation 2 from The Russian Revolution, 1900–1927 (Studies in European History), 4th ed, Palgrave Macmillan (Service, R.) p.75–6; Extract on page 129 in Interpretation 1 from Popular Opinion in Stalin's Russia, Cambridge University Press (Davies, S. 1997); Extract on page 129 in Interpretation 2 from An Economic History of the USSR, Penguin (Nove, A. 1989) pp.228–9, (Allen Lane The Penguin Press, 1969, Third edition, 1992) Copyright © Alec Nove, 1969, 1972, 1976, 1982, 1989, 1992; Extract on page 130 in Interpretation 3 from An Economic History of the USSR, Penguin (Nove, A. 1989) pp.385, (Allen Lane The Penguin Press, 1969, Third edition, 1992) Copyright © Alec Nove, 1969, 1972, 1976, 1982, 1989, 1992; Extract on page 131 in Interpretation 4 from The Great Fear: Stalin's Terror of the 1930s, OUP (Harris, J. 2016) p.136, by permission of Oxford University Press; Extract on page 134 in Interpretation 1 from A History of the Soviet Union, 1917–1991 Penguin (Hosking, G. 1992) p.213; Extract on page 134 in Source C from Everyday Stalinism: Ordinary Life in Extraordinary Times: Soviet Russia in the 1930s, OUP (Fitzpatrick, S. 1999) p.153, by permission of Oxford University Press; Extract on page 137 in Interpretation 2 from Women's Studies Encyclopedia, Volume 3, Greenwood Publishing Group (Tierney, H. 1999) p.1432 & p.1433; Extract on page 137 in Interpretation 3 from Political and Economic Encyclopaedia of the Soviet Union and Eastern Europe Longman (White, S. & Artesian, P. 1990) p.296.